Laughter tracked

EDITORIAL

by **Rachael Jolley**

When cartoonists are being arrested, and novelists told their plots must only support the government line, you know your nation is in deep trouble, argues **Rachael Jolley**

A COUNTRY'S SENSE OF humour is a nebulous thing. But when it starts to disappear, something serious is afoot.

And so it is in Spain right now. Comedy, it turns out, is touching a nerve, as it often does, and rather surprisingly the lawyers are getting involved. Comedy is not only a threat, but under threat.

What's bizarre is, this is Spain, a modern democracy, a solid, sensible country at the centre of Europe. Locking people up for making a joke, that's something you might expect from an authoritarian and struggling state. But Spain?

Well, it turns out, this is Spain in the 21st century. The list of comedy offences is not short. Spanish comedian Dani Mateo was told to testify before a judge in May for telling a joke referring to a monument built by Franco's regime as "shit". He told the joke during a satirical show. Now it doesn't sound like the best joke in the world, but hell, we defend his right to tell it. And Mateo is not alone in the Spanish comic fraternity. There's Facu Díaz, who was prosecuted last year for posting jokes on social media; Cassandra Vera, who was sentenced to a year in prison for making jokes about a former Spanish president; and three women who were accused of a religious hate crime for mocking a traditional Easter procession. Puppeteers whose Punch and Judy show included a sign for a made-up terrorist organisation carried by a witch spent a year fighting prosecution, unable to leave the country for weeks, receiving anonymous threats and having to report regularly to the police. On and on it goes, as Silvia Nortes reports for us on page 85.

So why does any of this matter? Well, jokes are a barometer of public mood, and as British comedian Andy Hamilton told this summer's Hay Festival, you can even use them to test how much the public like or dislike a politician or public figure. He remembered making a joke about then Prime Minister Margaret Thatcher, and being told by one of her staunchest supporters to expect a wave of outrage. On checking, he found just three complaints, and that's when, he said, he knew Thatcher was on the way out. Similarly, a recent joke about former UK Justice Secretary Michael Gove received a big fat zero moans in the BBC complaints box. Hamilton reckoned this was a sign of just how little the public cared about Gove.

So jokes do take the temperature of the nation, and one of many reasons politicians fear them is, as Mark Twain said, "Against the assault of laughter, nothing can stand."

Politicians fear being made fun of, and fear that a satirical representation of themselves may take root in the electorate's brain. They fear the public seeing their weaknesses. Some may remember that the classic satirical British TV puppet show Spitting Image reduced each member of →

CHIEF EXECUTIVE
Jodie Ginsberg

EDITOR, MAGAZINE
Rachael Jolley

EDITOR, ONLINE AND NEWS
Sean Gallagher

FINANCE DIRECTOR
David Sewell

DEPUTY EDITOR
Jemimah Steinfeld

ASSISTANT EDITOR, ONLINE AND NEWS
Ryan McChrystal

HEAD OF FELLOWSHIPS
David Heinemann

HEAD OF STRATEGIC EVENTS AND PARTNERSHIPS
Helen Galliano

HEAD OF ADVOCACY
Melody Patry

PROJECT OFFICER
Hannah Machlin

EDITORIAL ASSISTANT
Kieran Etoria-King

ADMINISTRATIVE ASSISTANT
Rosie Gilbey

ASSOCIATE PRODUCER
Julia Farrington

DIRECTORS & TRUSTEES
David Aaronovitch (Chair), Anthony Barling, Kate Maltby, David McCune, Turi Munthe, Sanjay Nazerali, Elaine Potter, David Schlesinger, Mark Stephens, Jason DaPonte, Kiri Kankhwende

PATRONS
Margaret Atwood, Simon Callow, Steve Coogan, Brian Eno, Harold Evans, Christopher Hird, Lord Joel Joffe, Jude Kelly, Michael Palin, Matthew Parris, Alexandra Pringle, Gabrielle Rifkind, Sir Tom Stoppard, Lady Sue Woodford Hollick

ADVISORY COMMITTEE
Julian Baggini, Clemency Burton-Hill, Ariel Dorfman, Rose Fenton, Michael Foley, Andrew Franklin, Conor Gearty, Andrew Graham-Yooll, AC Grayling, Lyndsay Griffiths, William Horsley, Anthony Hudson, Natalia Koliada, Jane Kramer, Htein Lin, Jean-Paul Marthoz, Robert McCrum, Rebecca MacKinnon, Beatrice Mtetwa, Julian Petley, Michael Scammell, Kamila Shamsie, Michael Smyth, Tess Woodcraft, Christie Watson

→ the cabinet to a single ridiculous idea, a spitting former Home Secretary Roy Hattersley or a tiny David Steel tucked in the top pocket of David Owen (joint leaders of the SDP-Liberal alliance). Not good for their egos, not good for their future prospects. Steel said later that the sketch definitely affected his image.

Joke-telling is not the only ingredient in the comedy cupboard that upsets the powers that be. Historically, exaggerated portraits, as Edward Lucie-Smith writes in issue 197 of Index on Censorship, have long been used to diminish or enhance a public character. The most obvious creators of exaggerated portraits are newspaper cartoonists, who sometimes feel the long arm of the police on their shoulders as a result.

In our exclusive interview with legendary South African cartoonist Zapiro, he talks not only about the power of cartoonists, but the pressure on them not to offend or upset. In an interview with South African journalist Raymond Joseph, Zapiro said: "We provoke thought, even if that thought is pretty outrageous. Others can do it too. We just occupy a space where you can really push the boundaries." Zapiro faced a six-year court battle with South Africa's President Jacob Zuma over one of his cartoons. But Zapiro is just as feisty as

Against the assault of laughter, nothing can stand

ever, and reckons he is bolshier than the generations that have come after him.

Cracking down on comedy is just one way to command and control society. This issue's special report examines others as we study the long shadows Russia's 1917 revolution cast within and without its national borders.

From the beginning the early Soviets were not particularly fond of disagreement. Shortly after their rise to power, between October

1917 and June 1918, around 470 opposition publications were closed down. Lenin was clear how the nation should work. He believed that journalists, novelists and opinion formers were either with him, or against the state. If they were against the state, they shouldn't be allowed to write or outline their views. "Down with non-partisan writers," he argued. This is a view very much in favour with many other rulers today, including Angola's President José Eduardo dos Santos, Chinese President Xi Jinping, and, recently, US President Donald Trump.

That idea of groupthink, honed by the Soviet Union, satirised by George Orwell, continues to haunt writers in former communist countries today. In Uzbekistan, as Hamid Ismailov outlines, the Soviet Union may have fallen, but the thinking remains the same. Writers with arguments that contradict President Shavkat Mirziyoyev are either neutralised by being employed by the state as advisers and consultants, or leave the country, or fail to be published.

CREDIT: Paul Brown/Rex/Shutterstock

LEFT: A Punch and Judy show in Covent Garden, London, where they have been performed for centuries. Recently Spanish puppeteers were prosecuted under terrorism legislation

In President Vladimir Putin's Russia most of the media, apart from a few brave exceptions, fall into line with government positions. For instance, in February this year, according to the Index-led Mapping Media Freedom project, major Russian national television channels abruptly reduced the number of times they mentioned the US president. This followed a Kremlin order to cut back on "fawning coverage" of Trump.

In all the recent furore over "fake news", prompted by almost incessant use of the term by Trump to undermine any reporting he didn't like, it's worth pointing out that tricks to get the public to believe something that is not true have been used throughout history. In fact, as Jemimah Steinfeld investigates (page 114), the Roman emperor Augustus was a master of manipulation well before PR handbooks were written.

And open the pages of a treasured book in our office and you'll see an early version of photoshopping at work. Photographs featured in The Commissar Vanishes: The Falsification of Photographs and Art in Stalin's Russia, show how people were "disappeared" from official Soviet portraits in the 1930s as they fell out of favour. Belarusians have been experiencing government attempts to get them to believe false stories for decades. In his report on page 52, Andrei Aliaksandrau unpicks the tricks used over the years and holds them up to the light.

And there's some excellent thoughtful pieces in our fiction section too, with two new short stories written for this publication: one by Turkish writer Kaya Genç, and the other by British writer Jonathan Tel. The final slice is a new English translation of a much older story, by Russia's "Comrade Count" Alexei Tolstoy.

To finish, a sad note. Our regular, and fantastic, Brazil correspondent Claire Rigby has died suddenly. Claire did amazing reporting for us, and we will miss her.

Rachael Jolley is the editor of Index on Censorship

CONTENTS

INDEX ON CENSORSHIP
VOLUME 46 NUMBER 02 – SUMMER 2017

Laughter tracked RACHAEL JOLLEY 1
Comedians are being locked up in Spain, but it's not the only country where having a laugh can get you in trouble

100 YEARS ON
WHAT DIFFERENCE RUSSIA'S REVOLUTION MAKES TO FREEDOM TODAY

Colouring inside the red lines BG MUHN ... 8
North Korea expert debunks myths and expectations about the country's art

Mexico's unlikely visitor DUNCAN TUCKER ... 12
Leon Trotsky might have arrived in Mexico with blood on his hands, but he quickly became a free speech fighter

The revolution will be dramatised
DAVID AARONOVITCH 16
Filmmaker Sergei Eisenstein manipulated the past in his work, but was it for dramatic or propaganda purposes?

A spectre that still haunts Russia
ANDREY ARKHANGELSKY 20
The Soviet fear of alternative voices persists in Russia

Lenin's long literary shadow
HAMID ISMAILOV 26
Uzbekistan's ruler still expects writers to conform

Land of milk and money LAHAV HARKOV 30
Israel's kibbutz movement walks a fine line between being harmonious and restrictive

Friends reunited KAYA GENÇ 34
For most of the 20th century, Turkey and Russia were hostile neighbours. Now, as both clamp down on free speech, they're finding common ground

The enemies of those people
NINA KHRUSHCHEVA 38
Nikita Khrushchev's great-grandchild considers life in Trump's USA compared to her Soviet upbringing

Airbrushing history
JEFFREY WASSERSTROM & YIDI WU 42
With China's Communist Party still in power, the way 1917 is remembered must follow the party line. One man learnt the hard way

Being the big man
RAFAEL MARQUES DE MORAIS 46
Angola's long-ruling president has constructed an image of himself straight out of Stalin's playbook

The big chill BERNARD GWERTZMAN 49
Staged press conferences and tapped phones were two obstacles to reporting from Moscow during the Cold War for The New York Times' correspondent

There's nothing new about fake news
ANDREI ALIAKSANDRAU 52
It might be a new term, but the mechanisms of fake news have been in place in Belarus for decades

Help! I'm a Taiwanese communist
MICHAEL GOLD **55**
Taiwan went through a mass killing of its communists. Today the country is opening up about this dark past and communists face a freer environment

Shot in Havana JAN FOX **58**
The state still controls Cuba's film industry, but a Cuban producer is hopeful about changes ahead

Global View JODIE GINSBERG **62**
Freedoms are being curtailed across the globe in the name of "national security"

IN FOCUS

Provoking the president
RAYMOND JOSEPH **66**
South African cartoonist Zapiro talks censorship and drawing in an exclusive interview

Yemen: "Nobody is listening to us"
LAURA SILVIA BATTAGLIA **70**
A Yemeni journalist discusses the time he was abducted for 15 days and other dangers for reporters

Novel lines JEMIMAH STEINFELD **73**
An interview with Margaret Atwood on current threats to free speech and why scientists need defending

No country for free speech?
DANIEL LEISEGANG **76**
An old libel law and a new one aimed at social media are two threats to free expression in Germany

Read all about it JULIA FARRINGTON **79**
Somaliland's hugely successful festival is marking 10 years of extending access to books

See no evil **82**
A Chechen journalist on the current climate of fear and intimidation that is stopping real news getting out

No laughing matter SILVIA NORTES **85**
Making jokes about Franco and ETA is off the table in Spain if you want to avoid trouble with the law

Cementing dissatisfaction
ELIZA VITRI HANDAYANI **87**
Indonesians experimenting with creative forms of protest are grabbing attention and sparking new movements

CULTURE

Frenemies KAYA GENÇ **92**
A mysterious man arrives at the White House. What does he want? A short story written exclusively for Index

Stitched in time JONATHAN TEL **98**
The award-winning writer on why the Chinese government controls historical narratives and an original story based on their ban of time travel shows

A tale of two Peters ALEXEI TOLSTOY **105**
First-time English translation of a story about Peter the Great by Russia's Comrade Count, Alexei Tolstoy

Index around the world
KIERAN ETORIA-KING **110**
A reporter from the Maldives explains why the Index 2017 awards were a much-needed boost

What the Romans really did for us
JEMIMAH STEINFELD **114**
When it comes to propaganda, Roman emperor Augustus was ahead of his time

---

EDITOR
Rachael Jolley
DEPUTY EDITOR
Jemimah Steinfeld
SUB EDITORS
Jan Fox, Tom Fearon, Sally Gimson, Adam Aiken, Alex Dudok de Wit
CONTRIBUTING EDITORS
Irene Caselli (Argentina), Jan Fox (USA), Kaya Genç (Turkey), Natasha Joseph (South Africa)

Index on Censorship | +44 (0) 20 7963 7262
292 Vauxhall Bridge Road, London SW1V 1AE, United Kingdom

EDITORIAL ASSISTANT
Kieran Etoria-King
DESIGN
Matthew Hasteley
COVER
Ben Jennings
THANKS TO
Jodie Ginsberg, Sean Gallagher, Ryan McChrystal
Magazine printed by Page Bros., Norwich, UK

SPECIAL REPORT

100 YEARS ON: WHAT DIFFERENCE RUSSIA'S REVOLUTION MAKES TO FREEDOM TODAY

Colouring inside the red lines BG MUHN ... 8

Mexico's unlikely visitor DUNCAN TUCKER ... 12

The revolution will be dramatised DAVID AARONOVITCH ... 16

A spectre that still haunts Russia ANDREY ARKHANGELSKY ... 20

Lenin's long literary shadow HAMID ISMAILOV ... 26

Land of milk and money LAHAV HARKOV ... 30

Friends reunited KAYA GENÇ ... 34

The enemies of those people NINA KHRUSHCHEVA ... 38

Airbrushing history JEFFREY WASSERSTROM AND YIDI WU ... 42

Being the big man RAFAEL MARQUES DE MORAIS ... 46

The big chill BERNARD GWERTZMAN ... 49

There's nothing new about fake news ANDREI ALIAKSANDRAU ... 52

Help! I'm a Taiwanese communist MICHAEL GOLD ... 55

Shot in Havana JAN FOX ... 58

MAIN: A Soviet propaganda poster from 1917

CREDIT: Heritage-Images/Art Media/akg-images

Colouring inside the red lines

46(02): 8/11 | DOI: 10.1177/0306422017715961

North Korea art expert **BG Muhn** goes behind the scenes to talk with the nation's artists and debunks some national stereotypes

CREDIT: Ji Zheng Tai/Mansudae Beijing

SPECIAL REPORT

OUTSIDE NORTH KOREA many people only know of the country's weapons testing and human rights violations. Given the common portrayal of a brainwashed society, many assume North Korean art is all state-ordered, uniform, functional and lacking artistic merit. But several recent exhibitions in both the UK and the USA have brought work from the Hermit Kingdom to the rest of the world and people's reaction to the art mirrors my own.

When I first went to North Korea to research the country's art I was totally stunned both by how art functions in the country and how good some of the work is. This was back in 2011. Now, nine trips later, I am still just as fascinated. Art is huge in North Korea. The biggest art exhibition, the National Art Exhibition, takes place in April every year in Pyongyang and attracts large crowds, though exact numbers are hard to come by. Many other government-sponsored exhibitions occur throughout the country. Some are for amateur artists and some are for professional artists.

Art is not just confined to exhibitions. It's on the streets, from the huge bronze statues of the "Great Leaders" and the →

ABOVE: Six artists lived and worked alongside construction workers for a month before painting The Miracle of Chongchon River

9
INDEXONCENSORSHIP.ORG

ABOVE: Clockwise from top left: North Koreans view paintings at the National Art Exhibition; a portrait of a worker; Yontan Shimwon Temple, an example of the little-known tradition of 'literary art'; a propaganda poster depicting Chollima, a mythical flying horse common in Korean culture

ubiquitous murals with slogans on them to propaganda posters pasted on buildings and billboard-like structures. And it's in people's homes. Some of this art is simply for aesthetics, but most serves a purpose, to reinforce citizens' ideas of patriotism and motivate them to do their best for the country.

As masters of the nation's ideology, artists are revered. They receive a decent salary and are often bestowed titles in recognition of good work. As a result, they face intense competition and years of training in order to be selected in a state-run studio, such as Mansudae Art Studio, the world's largest art studio with nearly 4,000 staff members.

North Korean art has its roots in Socialist Realism, the official Soviet art form institutionalised by Stalin. It veers away from the abstract. Kim Il Sung, first leader of North Korea, often said: "Art that people don't understand is not art." During my travels to Pyongyang, I spoke with a number of artists, including two highly respected artists, Choe Chang Ho and Kim In Sok. I asked Kim whether he knew about abstract art. He replied: "We know about that, but it doesn't fit with our society because people don't understand it." When I interviewed Choe about hyperrealism, a genre of painting or sculpture resembling a photo, his reply was similar to Kim's. "That kind of expression is unnatural and unpoetic, and therefore people will not be able to relate to it," he said.

In North Korea, few artists consider themselves propaganda tools. Propaganda art (*sonjonhwa*) comes under the umbrella of what is known as reproduction art (*chulpanhwa*). On top of this, paintings in oil, acrylic and traditional ink wash (*chosonhwa*) are categorised as fine art (*hwoihwa*).

Art has always occupied a central role in North Korea. After the Korean peninsula was divided into North and South in the 1950s, North Korea came under the influence of the Soviet Union. North Korean art was then significantly influenced by the Soviet Union. For example, in 1953 a Korean descendent in the Soviet Union, Varlen Pen, who was an artist and art professor at Repin Academy, was dispatched to Pyongyang and appointed dean of the Pyongyang Fine Arts University. He was tasked with educating

art students and faculty. Pen's influence was enormous. He instigated the tradition of "field sketching" or "direct rendering of objects", which has become part of art education in North Korea.

At the same time Kim Il Sung was consolidating his power against internal rivals and he started to distance North Korea from the Soviet Union. The concept of the *Juche* ideology was born. *Juche* ideology, which is commonly translated as "self-reliance", is central to North Korea. It blends the idea of the individual as the master of their own fate with the idea of the group as masters of the revolution. As part of the *Juche* ideology campaign, after Varlen Pen left in 1954, all the statues from the Soviet Union he used were destroyed and replaced with images of Koreans.

Since the mid-1950s, North Korean art has been saturated by the ideology of *Juche*. It means art is used as a vehicle to educate and motivate the people in line with the governmental policy, persuading them that the country's interests and their individual interests are one and the same.

Individual artists who are members of an art studio have a quota of paintings they must produce each month. Once they have submitted those works, they can spend time on their own art. Nevertheless, they stay within certain boundaries. Otherwise they face being ostracised from the art community, or worse. In the 1960s a well-established oil painter made the mistake of expressing the leader's image in a way that was deemed inappropriate and was forced to labour in a remote factory for 14 years. For many artists though, they wouldn't even consider painting the Kims in a negative light. They are seen as deities by most and people bow reverently at the statues and paintings of the leaders.

In addition to individual works, North Korean artists work collaboratively on huge paintings. When an event of import occurs, such as building a dam, a group of artists will go out to the area and will help with the project manually, all the while beginning to sketch images of the project, which will then form part of a wider collaborative work.

There is, surprisingly, some room for creativity. Over multiple visits to Pyongyang, I built working relationships with North Korean museum staff, state-run art studio officials, artists, as well as faculty members and students. As I scrutinised the art, particularly traditional ink wash painting on

For many artists though, they wouldn't even consider painting the Kims in a negative light

rice paper (*chosonhwa*), I found evidence, within circumscribed themes, of a high degree of creativity and skill. Looking at artworks at Mansudae Art Studio and Choson Art Museum, the mastery of brushstrokes and innovative solutions to artistic problems are evident. Within boundaries, I witnessed artists' passion to be creative, individual and to excel. In that sense, North Korean artists are not so different from artists anywhere else in the world. ⊗

*Born in South Korea, **BG Muhn** is an artist and art professor currently at Georgetown University. He is writing a book on North Korean art and curated an exhibition of North Korean Socialist Realism art last year in Washington*

BELOW: Two North Korean men look at a painting at the National Art Exhibition in Pyongyang

Mexico's unlikely visitor

With a new film about Trotsky's killing just released, **Duncan Tucker** looks at the history

DEEP, WIDE BULLET holes still mark the walls of the house where Leon Trotsky lived in exile in Mexico City's bohemian Coyoacán neighbourhood. Granted asylum two decades after leading the Russian Revolution of 1917, Trotsky spent his final years hiding from Soviet assassins and exhorting the importance of free press and artistic expression.

Responsible for the repression and murder of thousands of political opponents during Russia's Red Terror, Trotsky was an unlikely advocate for free speech. Yet, having been exiled by Joseph Stalin and airbrushed from Soviet history after losing out in a power struggle with his former comrade, he was no stranger to censorship himself.

Embraced by a small community of artists and intellectuals, Trotsky stayed active in Mexico, founding a local Marxist magazine and launching an international initiative for revolutionary art. Then he was murdered by a Stalinist agent.

A century on from the Russian Revolution and 80 years since Trotsky arrived in Mexico, his time there continues to pique →

RIGHT: Trotsky reads from Behind the Moscow Trial, a book examining Stalin's trials of Trotsky supporters, at his home in Mexico City in 1939

SPECIAL REPORT

public interest. His former home, now a museum, draws some 17,000 foreign visitors and 50,000 Mexican students a year, while The Chosen, a new film based on his assassination, was bought by Netflix and released in 190 countries in April.

Trotsky's presence in Mexico, a nation that had only emerged from its own decade-long revolution in 1920, proved divisive from the outset. The socialist-leaning president Lázaro Cárdenas had offered him asylum after Trotsky had difficult spells in Turkey, France and Norway, but the decision did not go down well with Mexico's Kremlin-backed communist party nor left-wing newspapers.

"Mexico's communist press attacked Trotsky systematically. They tried to have him expelled from Mexico and rejected by the labour movement," Dr Olivia Gall, author of the book Trotsky in Mexico, told Index. "They even tried to prepare public opin-

Trotsky spent his last years looking after his pet rabbits and trekking into the mountains

ion so that if Trotsky were assassinated it wouldn't cause too much drama in Mexico."

Trotsky stayed for two years with the iconic Mexican artists Diego Rivera and Frida Kahlo. He then moved a few blocks down the street after a political disagreement with the former and a rumoured affair with the latter. The first attempt on his life came in May 1940, when Stalinist agents sprayed his house with machine-gun fire.

"Awakened by the rattle of gunfire but feeling very hazy, I first imagined that a national holiday was being celebrated with fireworks outside our walls. But the explosions were too close, right here within the room, next to me and overhead," Trotsky wrote afterwards. "The odour of gunpowder became more acrid, more penetrating. Clearly, what we had always expected was now happening: we were under attack."

Trotsky and his wife survived by hiding beneath the bed while their bodyguards managed to repel the attackers. Yet his luck ran out just three months later, when another Soviet assassin stabbed him in the head with an ice pick while he was reading at his desk. Trotsky died the next day at the age of 60.

Covered with dusty books, ink pots and a metal lamp, Trotsky's wooden desk remains in his house, just as it was that day. His ashes lie in a stone tomb marked with a hammer and sickle in the leafy courtyard.

Known by those close to him as "the Old Man", Trotsky spent his last years looking after his pet rabbits and trekking into the mountains to pick rare flowers and cacti for his collection. He also still wrote prolifically.

In 1938 Trotsky founded Clave, a magazine that would circulate among small groups of Mexican Marxists. "Only the greatest freedom of expression can create favourable conditions for the advance of the revolutionary movement in the working class," Trotsky wrote in his first editorial. "The Mexican proletariat needs an honest press to express its needs, defend its interests, broaden its horizon and pave the way for the socialist revolution in Mexico. This is what Clave intends to do."

Debate over freedom of expression among Marxists in the turbulent 1930s was very different to what it is in many Western democracies today. "Trotsky argued that any attack on freedom of press was an attack on the worker's movement and socialist revolution. But he didn't see it as an attack on democracy, as we would today," Gall observed. "The central issue for the left was moving forward with the proletarian revolution, not whether socialist or communist projects should be democratic."

That year Trotsky also launched the International Federation of Independent Revolutionary Art alongside Rivera and the French

surrealist writer, poet and anti-fascist, André Breton. He and Breton co-wrote its manifesto, affirming that "in the realm of artistic creation, the imagination must escape from all constraint and must, under no pretext, allow itself to be placed under bonds."

Citing censorship in Nazi Germany and Soviet Russia, the authors warned of "the ever more widespread destruction of those conditions under which intellectual creation is possible." They emphasised the need for "complete freedom for art" and lamented that "thousands on thousands of isolated thinkers and artists are today scattered throughout the world, their voices drowned out by the loud choruses of well-disciplined liars."

Neither Clave nor the federation had the impact Trotsky desired. Breton helped the latter to gain ground in Europe, but momentum was lost after Rivera fell out with Trotsky and World War II broke out. Both initiatives came to an end shortly after Trotsky's death in 1940.

One of Trotsky's primary concerns was that censorship would leave the proletariat vulnerable to abuses of power. "Today the government may seem well disposed towards workers' organisations. Tomorrow it may fall, and it inevitably will, into the hands of the most reactionary elements of the bourgeoisie," he wrote in Clave. "In this case, the existing repressive laws will be used against the workers. Only adventurers who think of nothing but the moment's needs can fail to guard themselves against such a danger."

This proved to be the case in Mexico. Andrew Paxman, a historian at Mexico's Centre for Research and Teaching in Economics, told Index that Trotsky's vision for the Mexican press went unfulfilled as many worker-led newspapers closed down in the 1940s. Press freedom suffered as Mexico's ruling Institutional Revolutionary Party took a "right turn" and began clamping down on labour rights and co-opting the media through subsidies that encouraged self-censorship.

Throughout his time in Mexico Trotsky also had to confront what is now known as "fake news". The term may only have been popularised in the last year, but the way segments of the Mexican press covered Trotsky illustrated that there is nothing new about reporting falsehoods. Now-defunct newspapers such as El Popular and El Nacional portrayed Trotsky as a Nazi or US agent intent on stirring up trouble in Mexico, and

It was not, and still isn't, unusual for the powerful to use Mexico's press as a tool to attack or discredit rivals

even accused him of staging the shooting at his home, which left his grandson injured, in an attempt to provoke a war between the USA and Mexico. Trotsky identified his main aggressor as Vicente Lombardo Toledano, an influential labour leader who owned El Popular and had close links to the Kremlin.

It was not, and still isn't, unusual for the powerful to use Mexico's press as a tool to attack or discredit rivals. "There's a tradition in Mexican journalism that goes back to the 19th century of newspapers and magazines being set up not as businesses but as means of trafficking influence," Paxman noted. On top of sales, subscriptions and advertising revenue, he explained that they "have traditionally had two other revenue streams: the main one being government subsidies and the other being covert funding by a range of businessmen or politicians looking to boast about their deeds or defame rivals."

Trotsky did not have to wait long to demonstrate that the attacks and threats against him were genuine. Within just months of the botched shooting he was silenced forever.

Duncan Tucker is a freelance journalist based in Guadalajara, Mexico

The revolution will be dramatised

Influential Soviet director Sergei Eisenstein is often portrayed as the godfather of propaganda in film. **David Aaronovitch** argues that historical drama can also be manipulative when it ignores the past

MY FRIEND, A writer, reminded me of the English romantic poet John Keats's axiom that "we hate poetry that has a palpable design upon us". You could say, though, that Lenin and Mussolini – at least when it came to the poetry of film – knew differently. "Of all the arts, for us," said Lenin, "the cinema is the most important". "For us" meaning, of course, for the ruling Bolsheviks in the aftermath of the October 1917 revolution. When the Italian dictator Mussolini's new super studios were opened in 1936 a sign was erected over the gate reading "*Il cinema è l'arma più forte*", "cinema is the strongest weapon".

It was George Orwell, not a dictator (though they doubtless would smilingly have agreed with him) who wrote that, "he who controls the past controls the future. He who controls the present controls the past." It is pretty obvious that the way the powerful medium of film depicts the "then" has important implications for what people can be brought to believe about the "now".

I was brought up partly on films made in the Soviet Union and saw some of the most celebrated early movies when I was young. The director Sergei Eisenstein was the most famous name and before I was 12 I'd seen almost all his films, from the silent Strike made in 1924 to the extraordinarily ambivalent and terrifying two-part classic Ivan the Terrible. Every single one of them can be said to have had some kind of agenda that dovetailed – sometimes perfectly, sometimes awkwardly – with that of the Soviet state.

The two that were most obviously about Bolshevism and Russia were The Battleship Potemkin, dealing with events in the city of Odessa in 1905, and October, an account of the "ten days that shook the world" – the Bolshevik seizure of power – in Petrograd (St Petersburg) in 1917.

Both deploy Eisenstein's famous techniques of intercutting, juxtaposition and montage to create mood and drama. Sometimes cutaways of objects or expressions are inserted to refer obliquely to what the viewer is supposed to think of the person or the moment being depicted.

And in both films the actual history is bent for the purposes of the filmmaker. The massacre on the Odessa steps (once seen, never forgotten) from the movie Potemkin didn't actually happen. The film version of the storming of the Winter Palace in October

The massacre on the Odessa steps (once seen, never forgotten) from the movie Potemkin didn't actually happen

involved many more actors than the actual event itself. And October was criticised in Keatsian terms by no less a luminary than Lenin's widow, Nadezhda Konstantinovna Krupskaya. "Crude tricks will not do," she said. "The dead horse suspended over the water, hanging from the shafts of the opening bridge; the murdered woman's hair spreading out, covering the bridge's slats. It's too much like an advertisement, it's theatrical." It is, if you like, "palpable design".

But was it "propaganda" in the sense that Eisenstein's intention was primarily to make us believe something about the past? I'd say probably not. Any more than Mel Gibson messed around with the story of William Wallace for Braveheart for reasons other than to make a more dramatic movie.

Here let me introduce a film released last year in Russia called Panfilov's 28. This is a hero war movie about a legendary incident in World War II when 28 Red Army guardsmen held up an attack by Nazi tanks on

ABOVE: A poster for Sergei Eisenstein's 1925 film Battleship Potemkin

Moscow, destroyed dozens and died to a man. This was reported by Soviet newspapers at the time, but years later an opening of the archive showed that the story had been substantially manufactured for propaganda purposes. This problem did not deter the makers. "It's a movie, not a documentary," said the film's director when taxed with its inauthenticity.

As my writer friend (who is an American) also reminded me, a film director of a wartime epic or even a biopic, when it comes to sticking closely to real life, "gives a flying fuck in a rolling doughnut". If the narrative arc of a William Wallace picture requires an act of the coldest violence from its anti-hero, then out of the 10th floor castle window goes his son's gay lover.

No, Braveheart is not Scottish nationalist

But when did you last see a successful British movie dealing with the consequences of imperial rule?

propaganda, any more than Saving Private Ryan is American propaganda. Until, of course, it is shown at, say, a public meeting of Cumbernauld Young Nationalists. Then its intention is altered.

The capacity for context to matter can be illustrated by a speech made at the opening of Panfilov's 28 by the Russian minister of culture, Vladimir Mendinsky. His target was those who dared to criticise the movie's lack of historical accuracy. "It's our air," he told them, "our history, our culture. If you don't like it, don't breathe. Don't defile our air with your stench." The elision of accurate history and culture and the metaphysical air-that-we-breathe is a totalitarian formulation. And whatever the director originally thought he was doing, Mendinsky has turned it into something very different.

The Mendinsky approach to the representation of history is now all too familiar in eastern Europe. Since the Law and Justice Party came to power in Poland in 2015, for example, it has set about a form of historical "cleansing" of Poland's past, affecting the arts and museums.

We should allow a counter argument: is it possible that the messages, unconsciously or not, so deliberately conveyed about history, are just as propagandistic as those that are more obvious and intentioned. More, maybe, since not being "palpably designed" they are not as likely to be "hated"?

My dad thought so in his Stalinist period as the Communist Party's cultural secretary in the early 1950s. He saw "saccharine" songs and musicals of post-war Hollywood as conveying a consistent message designed to sell capitalism as the fulfilment of all human wishes. Funnily enough, 60 years on, my American writer friend kind of agrees. Once again there was no outright intention, but the effect was an idea of plenitude and harmony that bent reality out of shape.

And then there's omission. Sometimes in modern Britain you'd hardly believe that, until fairly recently, we had an empire. We believed we were entitled to rule other people and that they should submit to our rule. But when did you last see a successful British movie dealing with the consequences of imperial rule? Is absence also possibly a form of propaganda? ⊗

David Aaronovitch is a journalist, author and chair of Index on Censorship

Your Essential Guide to the Best music from Around the World

"Music, more than words or literature, has a power to transcend borders and move people. It makes it a very powerful medium, and this is why musicians are so often the target of censorship. *Songlines* magazine is all about politics, history and identity, and the artists who incite change through their music."

Simon Broughton, *Songlines* **editor-in-chief**

SUBSCRIBE AND CLAIM YOUR FREE CD

SONGLINES MAGAZINE

Find out more at www.songlines.co.uk/songhoyblues or call 0800 137 201

Full annual retail price for print only (10 issues) is £59.50; One-year subscription £49.50 UK, £68.20 EU, £71.80 ROW. Postage and packaging is included. Quote 'Index' when ordering on the phone. Your CD will be sent within 30 days of receiving payment.

A spectre that still haunts Russia

Moscow-based writer **Andrey Arkhangelsky** looks back at 1917 and says that Soviet attitudes to debate persist in Russia today

IMMEDIATELY AFTER THE October Revolution, on 27 October 1917, the Bolshevik government issued one of its first decrees: the decree on the press. This required all newspapers critical of the Soviets to be silenced, and on the basis of that decree, between October 1917 and June 1918, more than 470 opposition newspapers were closed down or otherwise ceased to exist. The tsarist autocracy had also attempted to restrict press freedom in Russia prior to 1917, but it had not denied the very right of the press to criticise the authorities. Between 1901 and 1916, 14,000 periodicals of various political persuasions were published in Russia, 6,000 of them in St Petersburg and Moscow. The eminent Estonian professor Pavel Reifman once wrote that censorship in pre-revolutionary Russia was harsh, but "in the Soviet Union it assumed a new quality: it became all-encompassing, all-powerful". The new regime banned, as a matter of principle, the right to hold a point of view different from that of the regime. In the opinion of the late Russian historian, Alexander Nekrich, the aim of Soviet censorship was "to create a new collective memory in the population".

Nobody could have imagined the impact this decree would have on the psychology of Soviet citizens. For the authoritarian mindset, it is normal to have just one point of view, uniquely correct, that always coincides with the opinion of the regime and one's superiors. There is an even more radical corollary underlying this: the right to exercise

RIGHT: Police walk past a monument of Lenin after a rally to support then presidential candidate Vladimir Putin in 2012. The banner in the background reads "Our vote is for Putin!"

CREDIT: Sergei Karpukhin/Reuters

physical and symbolic force against the individual. For the Soviet regime this axiom became not just a tool but an outlook, a fundamental principle. The ban was not just on writing or speaking out of turn, it was a prohibition on being different, of not being identical to everybody else.

For all the might of its suppressive apparatus, the Soviet regime continued to be terrified of the slightest freedom of expression, and it put a great deal of energy into crushing it. Indeed, as subsequently became evident, the Soviet ideal could exist only in a hermetically sealed, self-contained space. The

As subsequently became evident, the Soviet ideal could exist only in a hermetically sealed, self-contained space

situation was like that in the fairytale about an evil princess who ordered all mirrors to be removed from her palace in order not to see her pimple. You can get by without a mirror for years, decades even, but when one accidentally finds its way into the palace, the impact is devastating. That is what happened to the Soviet regime: as soon as the gates of *perestroika* were opened, even slightly, between 1986 and 1991. As soon as there was scope for differences of opinion, the Soviet project found itself unable to survive for even another six years. The foundations of a massive building labelled '"socialism" were undermined by a puny trickle of free discussion, the very thing banned in 1917.

The USSR ceased to exist, but homo sovieticus was still around. The paradox was registered between 1994 and 1999 by the Yury Levada Analytical Centre (now the Levada Centre) that the Soviet mentality persisted.

Soviet Man finds the very possibility of having a choice disturbing. Russian Federation propaganda, describing elections in

The present regime in Russia replicates this principal feature of Bolshevism: it despises the other person's opinion

Europe where there is no knowing right up until the last minute which of the candidates will win, successfully persuades him that this is a shortcoming, not the whole point of the system and that it is dangerous.

For most of the Russian population, press freedom is of little interest: they think it is something of concern only to journalists. President Vladimir Putin tapped into this mood and from the early 2000s he rearranged the media in Russia along Soviet lines, concentrating particularly on television: all the main television channels now reflect only the point of view of the regime. Putin has, admittedly, learned some lessons from the experience of the USSR, and leaves just a chink of freedom for a number of print publications, a couple of radio stations (Echo of Moscow and Radio Liberty) and a single television channel (Rain) which, for the time being at least, are able to express views not in harmony with those of the authorities.

Restricting free speech is typical of an authoritarian regime, but by doing so, the present regime struck a body blow at a society that was only just beginning to acquire the skills of dialogue and communication. The authorities in Russia simply do not understand what those are and see no value in them. They see dialogue only as a means of manipulation, but it involves a lot more than merely opening and closing your mouth; it has to involve a readiness to "wait for the other", as the philosopher Paul Ricoeur put it. Dialogue involves a readiness to "accept the world", to take account of it. That is what meaningful communication is and it is the only way to smooth out, at least to some extent, the unavoidable cultural gap between different people.

In Russia, "dialogue" is understood as a synonym for fighting and you are justified in using all necessary means to defeat your adversary. We can illustrate this with the example of any political talk show on the Russian federal channel, where the regime's apologists gang up to attack lone opponents, not allowing them to get a word in edgewise; or with the kind of language recently used by Vladimir Safrokov, Russia's representative in the United Nations, when he told the British ambassador: "Look at me when I am talking to you," in a row over Russia's support for the Syrian regime of Bashar al-Assad.

Contempt for dialogue, for meaningful communication, is the main psychological consequence of the censorship introduced in 1917, because censorship not only prohibits the expressing of a different opinion, it actively trains us not to discuss, not to listen to an opponent, not to respect his rights, not to take account of him as a person. The present regime in Russia replicates this principal feature of Bolshevism: it despises the other person's opinion; it prefers the use

CREDIT: Martin Rowson

ABOVE: A man protests government corruption in St Petersburg in March 2017. His sign reads: "St Petersburg is a city of poets and free thinkers, we should protect it from barbarians and witch hunters"

→ of force (in the case of Safrokov, only psychological). However, this atrophying of elementary communication skills is coming back to haunt the regime, as is evident, for example, in the clumsy attempt to demolish dilapidated, Khrushchev-era residential blocks in Moscow and replace them with new buildings. One might imagine this would be cause for celebration, but the authorities communicated with the people affected in the tones of a camp commandant haranguing his subordinates, a lack of respect that caused predictable resentment. Why not just enter into dialogue with the residents involved? Why not give them a say? The Russian regime would, however, feel it was lowering itself if it were to seek agreement with other people. It is accustomed to issuing orders, to dictating terms, and this rejection of dialogue becomes the norm. We see the same thing in the failed dialogue between teachers and their pupils, which appeared on the internet on the eve of, and in the aftermath of, the anti-corruption protests on 26 March this year.

A new generation of pupils and students, born when Putin was already in power, ask their teachers questions about corruption, which the teachers are incapable of answering. They can only accuse the pupils of treason and mouth clichés from the Soviet era. The pupils are familiar with social networks and accustomed to dialogue and alternative sources of information, while their teachers, who only watch TV and consider the internet "trash", fail to find a common language with them. Moreover, they have no wish to do so. The two generations seem to speak entirely different languages and this results from the deficit of meaningful communication within society. It is just the way things became in the Soviet Union of the 1980s, when the gap between Soviet reality and Soviet propaganda became enormous.

CREDIT: Farhad Sadykov/Flickr

Life without a mirror generates a hermetic, self-contained mentality in which Russia is always right, while the rest of the world is stupid and ridiculous. The world is incapable of judging Russia fairly, of appreciating how beautiful and intelligent we Russians are. The world is jealous of us and wants to destroy us. The lack of a mirror generates a perverse morality that ignores universal values, believing that only what we say is true; only our understanding of good and evil is correct. This too is a legacy of 1917, when truth, good and moral values had to come with the prefix "Soviet". This is a morality with no faith in individuals, in their ability to accomplish anything of their own free will. It is a morality that claims the various "colour revolutions" happened "at the behest of the West", and that any human passion can be explained in terms of nothing more exalted than personal gain.

Finally, the lack of a culture of pluralism has once more made possible manipulation of the population through television, on a massive scale. A monstrous propaganda experiment was conducted after the protests of 2014, which seems beyond belief in the 21st century: how, given that there is an internet with thousands of alternative sources of information, can people believe only what they are told on television? Alas, we have to recognise this as a feature of authoritarian thinking, which finds it unacceptable for there to be an alternative point of view. People with this mindset are used to living in a world where decisions about what is good and what is evil are taken on their behalf by the state, to which they entrust their consciences. No one today is prohibiting them from seeking an alternative point of view, but that is not something they want. For such a person, there is no problem if the regime completely changes its mind from one day to the next, as in George Orwell's novel 1984. Yesterday Turkey was an enemy and today it is a friend, because that is what Big Brother has decided.

The regime has, however, come up against a paradox. This kind of psychology is incompatible with Russia's economic model which, so far at least, is still capitalist and founded on private property. There is no understanding that a modern economy is not based on oil and gas alone but, more importantly, on communication, on respect for others, on tolerance. A modern economy can be built only with people who know how to compromise, with the daily input of the individual decisions of millions, as economist Friedrich von Hayek argued. Only a culture of pluralism, only freedom of speech can educate people to be capable of taking such decisions. We have run up against a brick wall. It is impossible to build an efficient economy with unfree people. Free people, however, are just what the Putin regime most fears. It

Life without a mirror generates a hermetic, self-contained mentality in which Russia is always right

will permit no changes; it is a dead end and, like the Soviet regime before it, is gradually pushing itself into a corner, trapping itself, by underestimating human psychology.

The roots of this impasse are to be found right there, in 1917. That is when it all began, with the prohibition of free speech, the prohibition of free thought. The shadow of 1917 hangs over Russia to this day and it seems, alas, that the country has failed to learn the lesson given by the USSR. Today that ban on free speech is again leading Russia up the same path, to the same dead end, with no sign of a way out.

Translated by **Arch Tait**

Andrey Arkhangelsky *is a Russian writer, who regularly contributes to* Index on Censorship *magazine*

Lenin's long literary shadow

Lenin's argument that all fiction is political still influences the way the Uzbek government considers writers, argues novelist **Hamid Ismailov**

IN SOVIET TIMES the Lenin monument in the capital of Uzbekistan, Tashkent, was possibly the biggest in the world. Once, on the eve of the anniversary of the October Revolution, as I was passing, I witnessed the cleaning of that monument. A climber was perched on Lenin's eyelashes, jet-washing his enormous forehead, and another was almost out of sight inside his ear. After the break-up of the USSR, the monument was sold abroad and in its place the Uzbek authorities erected, on the same pedestal, a huge globe with only one country on it. Guess which one? Obviously this was the newly independent Uzbekistan. The old Lenin Square was renamed Mustaqillik Maydoni, (Independence Square). Yet paraphrasing what was stated in The Communist Manifesto, I could say the following about the replacement monument: "A spectre is haunting the globe, the spectre of Lenin."

Replacing monuments on the same pedestal is in fact a metaphor for the whole process of replacing communist ideology with the ideology of *mustaqillik* (independence) over the last 25 years. Though on the surface the Uzbek authorities tried very hard to show their resolve to get rid of the communist past, what they built instead stands on the same foundations.

Lenin's argument that all literature is political still defines the Uzbek authorities' attitudes and the way writers themselves see their role in society today.

Bolshevik ideology that defines the role of literature is based on Lenin's articles, written between 1906 and 1911, with the main one being Party Organisation and Party Literature. There he wrote: "Down with non-partisan writers! Down with literary supermen! Literature must become part of the common cause of the proletariat, 'a cog and a screw' of one single great social democratic mechanism set in motion by the entire politically conscious vanguard of the entire working class. Literature must become a component of organised, planned and integrated social democratic party work." Lenin continued: "Publishing and distributing centres, bookshops and reading-rooms, libraries and similar establishments must all be under party control."

Rejecting previous literature as hypocritical and bourgeois, Lenin finally proclaimed his vision of, "a truly free one that will be openly linked to the proletariat". Everything beyond that was obviously severely censored.

When I first read this article in my twenties, I was horrified, because my writing was not "openly linked to the proletariat" at →

ABOVE: A celebration in Tashkent's Lenin Square, Uzbekistan, for the 50th anniversary of the October Revolution in 1967. The Lenin monument was removed in 1992

→ all. It was about myself and it took 10 years for my first collection of "decadent" poems, Garden, to be published in Tashkent, in 1987. My book of poetry got through the censors, because it was cushioned with a preface by an acclaimed, but liberal writer, who argued that even Soviet poetry needed some whispering voices alongside it, like the background cries heard in bazaars. On top of that, my smart and cunning editor added titles to my poems such as, To the Great Patriotic Widows, though what I had written had nothing to do with war or patriotism.

A hundred years after Lenin, the first president of independent Uzbekistan, Islam Karimov, in an article devoted to the role of literature in society, also rejected the previous epoch's writing, this time Uzbek Soviet literature. He said: "It should be noted that most of the writers were brought up by the

CREDIT: akg-images/Sputnik

Soviet era. For many years, they worked under that dominant ideology. But the truth is, though many of them seemingly approved of the ideas of the communist regime, in their hearts they did not accept those ideas."

Talking about the role of writers and their work in the new Uzbekistan, however, he nearly repeated Lenin's maxim about the relationship between literature and society. He wrote: "Since our writers have assumed the great, difficult and complex responsibility of raising, through their talents, the consciousness and outlook, the cultural level of the people, it is for them, first of all, vitally important that they feel profoundly their civic responsibility towards the nation, like a child in front of parents." Once again, what doesn't fit into this definition is ruthlessly censored.

Remember what I said about the replacement globe on the pedestal: "A spectre is haunting the globe, the spectre of Lenin?"

As in any traditional society, it is literature that has played the role of public consciousness in Uzbekistan, and the same literature prepared the ground for the creation of the new *mustaqillik* ideology. However, after this ideology was adopted by the state, Uzbek literature found itself in disarray. The shrewdest writers and poets turned out to be the ones who had, in Soviet times, written poems and novels about the party and Lenin, and who then found it easy to bring their work in line with the new ideology by replacing the party with the nation, and Lenin with Amir Timur (the great medieval conquerer fictionalised in Christopher Marlowe's play as Tamburlaine), or at worst with the president. They found that this literature was, and still is, in demand. The new lyrics of the Uzbek national anthem are the epitome of this, with its melody left unchanged from the Soviet time, just like how the monument of the globe in the newly named Independence Square still stands on the same foundations.

It has been more difficult for writers and poets with a literary-nationalist streak who had feelings of dissent during the Soviet era. The subject of their dissidence has now become a state ideology, therefore some of them were recruited from the ranks of the opposition to the current ruling party, writing books like Feeling of Motherland: an Encyclopaedia of Uzbekness. A few others, for whom literature was a higher notion than current politics, were forced to emigrate, like Muhammad Solih, Nurulloh Muhammed Raufxon, Yusuf Juma, Xoldor Vulqon and Jahongir Muhammad, or go into internal exile like the late poet Rauf Parfi, the novelist Salomat Vafo and the poet known simply as Shukrullo.

Even Soviet poetry needed some whispering voices alongside it, like the background cries heard in bazaars

So the process of creating and implementing the ideology of independence in Uzbekistan has been pursued with more utilitarian and pragmatic goals, and in general repeated the communist totalitarian system of ideological governance. If you replace, let's say, the emblematic figure of Lenin with Amir Timur, or the idea of communism with the idea of nationalism, the philosophy of dialectical materialism with Sufism, the function of these elements in society and the state remain essentially the same. Their essence is the ideology of total control from top down and writers and poets are still seen as "cogs and screws" in the hands of those who are in power. Thus, the famous words of the writer Vladimir Mayakovsky: "Lenin lived, Lenin lives, Lenin will live forever", ring true, hidden like a ghost behind the globe with at least one country on it. ⊗

Hamid Ismailov is an Uzbek writer and journalist. His books are banned in Uzbekistan

Land of milk and money

As a controversial high-rise complex is planned in a large Israeli kibbutz, **Lahav Harkov** examines how open to challenge and discussion these supposedly egalitarian communities are

ISRAEL'S KIBBUTZ MOVEMENT promised a utopian ideal where people would live together in an equal, communal environment, but the reality wasn't always democratic or open to debate. Once traditional agricultural enclaves, the modern kibbutz is more cosmopolitan and less collectivist.

Ma'agan Michael, a Mediterranean beachfront commune 30 kilometres south of Haifa, will be the first kibbutz to have a high-rise apartment building. A plan to build a high-rise addition, to make more room for married children of kibbutz members and their families, recently raised concerns it would erode communitarian ideals. In the spirit of egalitarianism, it came down to a vote; the new building was approved.

Over the years, kibbutzim have been influenced by broader national social and economic reforms. Many have changed to keep pace with Israel's more individualistic society.

"There is a saying by [philosopher] Martin Buber that when you look at the slogans of the French Revolution – liberté, égalité, fraternité – the West took the freedom and forgot the equality, while the East took the equality and forgot the liberty, and everyone forgot the fraternity," Muki Tsur, a historian and former secretary-general of the kibbutz movement, told Index. "The idea of the kibbutz was that through fraternity, you can have freedom and equality together. People united out of free will to have equality between them."

According to Tsur, this idea "created an infrastructure for freedom of expression". The traditional kibbutz model, under which everyone is equal, encouraged open dialogue at communal meetings. If an argument concerned an issue that had a practical impact on the kibbutz, a vote was generally held. And since the kibbutz was entirely voluntary, people could leave if they seriously disagreed with the result of a vote or chafed against the social conformity.

"Leaving is also part of freedom of expression," Tsur said.

Yet the pressure to conform undermined free expression for many members. For example, for decades there was one shared pool of clothing for each gender in most kibbutzim.

"Take any small town in the world and there will be a strong base of conformity," Tsur said.

In Yael Neeman's book We Were the Future, a memoir of life on a kibbutz in

northern Israel in the 1960s and 1970s published last year, she shows the idealism of kibbutz life, but also the terms of the project: religion was banned in most (though there was a separate Orthodox kibbutz movement); jobs were allocated; and communal activities were mandatory. In some kibbutzim, children lived separately from parents – an attempt to bypass the nuclear family – and would be submitted to sessions where they learnt about the evils of capitalism. Hence, the kibbutz's unfolding happened partly because people demanded more freedom and individualism.

There were differences between kibbutzim

Take any small town in the world and there will be a strong base of conformity

and communes in a broader sense, too. The simple fact that the kibbutz movement was the spearhead of Zionism, requiring members to speak Hebrew in public spaces in an effort to build a Jewish national home, was a major divergence from the Soviet interpretation of a stateless, borderless order.

That didn't prevent the kibbutz's political representatives, including first Israeli →

ABOVE: Children at a kibbutz in Beit She'an valley in northern Israel, 1967

→ Prime Minister and Sde Boker kibbutz member David Ben-Gurion, from expressing identification with the Soviet Union at certain points. The far left United Workers' Party (Mapam), which included the left flank of the kibbutz movement, called the USSR "the second homeland".

However, Ben-Gurion moved towards a more Western orientation even before the State of Israel was established in 1948. The final straw, which split Mapam and left Soviet supporters as a tiny minority among kibbutzniks, was the Slánský Trial and Doctors' Plot in 1952 and 1953 that resulted in a purge of Jews in the Soviet Union. The Mapam split was a prominent but rare instance of people being expelled from a kibbutz because of political opinions, when Soviet supporters were no longer welcome.

The fall in kibbutz numbers has occurred in tandem with a move to the political right

The kibbutz movement was always a minority among Israelis. At its height, only 7% of Israeli Jews were members. Today, the kibbutz movement is far from what the 11 men and women who founded the first kibbutz, Degania Alef, in 1909 envisioned. At a political level, kibbutznik parliamentarians have dropped from 20 in the first Knesset to just one today. The change is more democratic, said Tsur, noting their political representation reflects the small minority kibbutzniks make up in Israeli society.

The fall in kibbutz numbers has occurred in tandem with a move to the political right in Israel. Dov Henin is the only Jewish parliamentarian in the Knesset who identifies as communist, though he is not a member of a kibbutz. He told Index he felt he could express communist views freely.

"I think today there is a greater space to express things than in the past, but at the same time they are the stances of a smaller minority," Henin said. "On socioeconomic issues, the fact that [far] left-wing criticism is from a small minority makes it less dangerous to the establishment, so it bothers them less."

Tsur pointed out that the left-right divide in Israel is less about socioeconomic issues and more about views on the Palestinian conflict. That's where issues of free speech, especially on the margins of Israeli society and politics, come into play. Henin implied as much, saying that "the establishment", which he used to refer to anyone to his political right, sees criticism on diplomatic and security issues as "dangerous". Reactions are more aggressive because "these criticisms are attacked much more than socioeconomic ones", he added.

Back in Ma'agan Michael, the new apartment block should be completed within five years. Even though Ma'agan Michael is considered by many as a kibbutz that has remained close to the movement's ideals, with shared property and a communal dining hall, it would probably be unrecognisable to those who founded it 68 years ago. ⊗

Lahav Harkov is the Knesset reporter for The Jerusalem Post and an international commentator and lecturer on Israeli politics and democracy. Follow her @LahavHarkov

International Contemporary Writing

Issue 89, Spring 2017

Wasafiri encourages readers and writers to travel the world via the word. For over three decades, we have created a dynamic platform for mapping new landscapes in contemporary international writing featuring a diverse range of voices from across the UK and beyond. Committed to profiling the 'best of tomorrow's writers today' we simultaneously celebrate those who have become established literary voices, offering a creative space for dialogue and debate.

www.wasafiri.org
@wasafiri1
www.facebook.com/wasafiri.magazine
www.wasafiri.org/new-writing-prize/

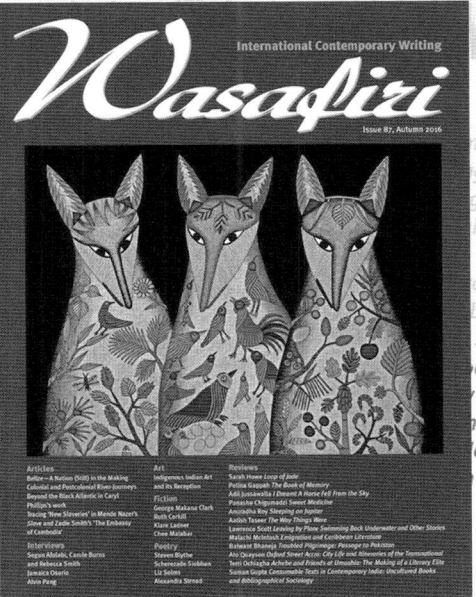

Friends reunited

Throughout the 20th century, Turkey's border with Russia made it an ideal military base for the anti-Soviet bloc. But now NATO's second largest military power is becoming one of Russia's greatest allies, **Kaya Genç** reports

ON THE CENTENARY of the Russian revolution, Turkey and Russia have become best friends once again. It's been a long and complex journey.

Nearly a year ago, on 27 June 2016, Vladimir Putin received a letter of apology from his Turkish counterpart about a Russian attack aircraft being downed by a Turkish F-16 fighter jet.

President Recep Tayyip Erdogan wrote about his regret for the death of the Russian pilot, the diplomatic kerfuffle that followed and the damage caused to trade and tourism ties between countries. The apology and material compensation offered in the letter were coupled with a wish for closer ties in the future.

At the moment of their creation, these two countries were close allies. Istanbul's Taksim Square, a few metres away from Gezi Park, the site of 2013's environmentalist protests, is dominated by the Republic Monument. This huge sculpture features the figures of Kliment Voroshilov, a Soviet marshal, and Mikhail Frunze, one of the leaders of the October Revolution, standing behind Mustafa Kemal Atatürk, the founder of modern Turkey. In the 1910s, Atatürk had been an ardent supporter of the Russian Revolution. As an Ottoman career soldier, he had seen the Russian uprising as part of the struggle of the eastern world against the oppressive West.

The Turkish republic's youthful love for the Soviets, which explains current day Turkish communists' admiration for Atatürk, proved to be a brief affair. Under the reign of his successor, İsmet İnönü, the Turkish regime shifted its alliances towards Nazi Germany. Then the single party regime of the Republican People's Party imprisoned communist sympathisers, and came very close to entering World War II on the German side. In fact, paranoia about the influence of Soviet culture was the original cause of Turkish state oppression.

Throughout the late 1930s and early 1940s, the first generation of Turkish dissidents, including novelists and poets, rebelled against the class system inherent to the Kemalist regime, taking their inspiration from Soviet revolutionaries. Under the single party rule of the Republican People's Party, Soviet sympathisers were ruthlessly prosecuted. In 1938, two years after Atatürk's death, three of Turkey's four greatest authors were behind bars for their pro-Soviet views: Orhan Kemal, Kemal Tahir and Nazım Hikmet. A fourth writer, Sabahattin Ali, was prosecuted for his communist sympathies. Ali, whose novel Madonna in a Fur Coat was published as a Penguin Classic last year, was murdered by a state agent on Turkey's border with Bulgaria while attempting to escape to the USSR.

During the 1950s, with Turkey's entry into NATO and the election of Prime Minister Adnan Menderes in the country's first free elections, Turkey again became an enemy of its neighbour, this time on nonfascist, pro-Western grounds. But it was during the much more recent premiership of Ahmet Davutoğlu, the architect of Turkey's interventionist foreign policy in Syria, that Turkey had its worst moments with Russia. "I have personally given the order to down the Russian plane," Davutoğlu boasted after the incident in 2015.

"Turkish sympathy and antipathy towards Russia have always been equally powerful," Sabri Gürses, Turkey's leading Russian to Turkish literary translator, told Index.

I believe it's miraculous that classical Russian literature is highly valued in Turkey

"The situation in Russia is probably the same. This is like being in a family, maybe being in the family Karamazov. Some members are more favoured at times and there is always tension in the house. What we lived through with the downing of the jet last year was that the antipathy found a leak in the system and tried to define the relationship."

Gürses, who translated books by Andrei Bely, Mikhail Bulgakov, Vladimir Nabokov and Svetlana Alexievich into Turkish, belongs to the latest generation of Turkey's Russian translators whose work has proved crucial in bringing together the two cultures in the past century. Most of Turkey's great Russian translators had been career soldiers trained at NATO missions, their Russian skills intended to serve anti-Soviet objectives.

These translators' mastery of Russian culture unexpectedly produced among them →

OPPOSITE: The Republic Monument in Istanbul's Taksim Square, which includes Bolshevik leaders Mikhail Frunze and Kliment Voroshilok in the crowd behind Mustafa Kemal Ataturk

CREDIT: Mel Longhurst/akg-images

a love for their purported enemy. Such figures became socialists and were eventually purged from the army, particularly in the wake of a failed coup attempt in 1971. Ergin Altay and Mehmet Özgül, both former career soldiers who studied at Kuleli Military Academy, which was closed down after the failed coup attempt in 2016, had translated Russian classics by Leo Tolstoy and Fyodor Dostoyevsky into Turkish.

The antipathy between the two nations have their roots in history. Ottomans were a threat and balancing power for Russia throughout the 19th century; Russians supported the independence of Balkans and then invaded Anatolia, erecting a statue on the coast of the

Novelists and poets have joined the ranks of those being prosecuted, accused of trying to undermine the state

Bosphorus, which was later destroyed.

"This strained history left traces in the national and individual memory of Turks, and didn't leave the Turkish mind during the 20th century when Soviet threat was real," Gürses, the translator, said. "So I believe it's miraculous that classical Russian literature is highly valued in Turkey. We have Russian classics at schools in the curriculum. Every student knows her Dostoyevsky, Pushkin, Tolstoy and even Gorky, but this is not the case in Russia. They have just learned about Orhan Pamuk. Nazım Hikmet and Reşat Ekrem affected them, but they are not so popular nowadays. And this was the most unfortunate thing; we didn't have much to balance the Russian antipathy against Turkey after the downing of the jet. Even Orhan Pamuk did not have much to say after the event. For ordinary Russians, Turkey is a place to live, to go on holiday, [in places like] Istanbul, Antalya, Bodrum. This is not enough."

After the downing of the jet, Russian cultural centres connected to Turkish culture were closed and Turkish students living in Russia had their visas cancelled. "I thought: What would happen if this family fell apart?" Gürses said. "Would I see in my lifetime Dostoyevsky's St. Petersburg or Tolstoy's Yasnaya again? Hopefully I would. It's difficult to describe how happy I would be to sit under the Pushkin statue in Moscow again."

Many Turkish authors, who have long held a passion for Russian literature, felt similar anxieties. "Gogol, Chekhov, Pushkin, Dostoyevsky, Tolstoy, Turgenev and later on Mayakovsky, Anna Akhmatova all played an important role in my literary and intellectual journey ever since I was a high school student in Turkey," the Turkish novelist Elif Şafak told Index. "Their concerns felt very familiar, their conflicts and quandaries pertinent to a place, and a region, yet also surprisingly universal."

With the newly established closer relationship with Russia, Turkey has gone some way to undoing the damage to its economy, and renewed its tourism ties.

But in today's Turkey, writers like Şafak are suffering the kind of political oppression their Russophile literary ancestors experienced in 1940s Turkey. Novelists and poets have joined the ranks of those being prosecuted, accused of trying to undermine the state.

"Both Turkey and Russia come from traditions of empire, and to a certain extent continue to have 'imperial dreams' and a romanticised, nationalistic notion of the past," Şafak said. "In both places writers lack the luxury of being apolitical. In both places, the individual freedoms are squandered under a strong, pervasive, aggressive state ideology… The biggest challenge for writers, past and present, Turkish and Russian, is to carve out a niche of freedom within top-down, pseudo-democratic regimes." ⊗

Kaya Genç is a contributing editor for Index on Censorship magazine, based in Istanbul, Turkey

JOURNALISTS REPORTED **42** ATTACKS TO PROPERTY IN Q2 2016.

Mapping Media Freedom collated and verified a total of 341 reports of violations of press freedom across Europe and neighbouring countries between April and June 2016 (Q2). The platform was founded by Index on Censorship in May 2014. You can read the latest report at Mappingmediafreedom.org

Xindex — the voice of free expression

EFJ | European Federation of Journalists

REPORTERS WITHOUT BORDERS FOR PRESS FREEDOM

CO-FUNDED BY THE European Commission

The enemies of those people

Khrushchev's great-granddaughter **Nina Khrushcheva** now lives in the USA. Here she talks about growing up in the former Soviet state and her fears for the future role of the US press

ABOVE: Traditional Russian dolls with pictures of Vladimir Putin, Vladimir Lenin and Donald Trump are sold at a fair in Red Square, Moscow

EVERY REGIME FROM the Romans to the French during the 1789 revolution to the Nazis and to the Soviets has dubbed those who disagreed with their often-brutal ideology as the "enemy of the people". Journalists have habitually topped the "enemy" lists, censored, harassed, injured, even killed just for doing their job – speaking truth to power, challenging the narratives of the supremacy of the rulers. Democracies normally have known better. Even George W. Bush, not the most liberal of US presidents, recently said: "Power can be very addictive…and it's important for the media to call to account people who abuse their power, whether it be here or elsewhere."

Enter the flashy property tycoon Donald Trump and the USA has joined the not so savoury club of the non-democrats. In February, the newly minted US president tweeted, "The FAKE NEWS media (failing @nytimes, @NBCNews, @ABC, @CBS, @CNN) is not my enemy, it is the enemy of the American People!" Many shivered in disbelief: A verbal déjà vu of the Nazi propaganda minister Joseph Goebbels, who dubbed the Jews the "sworn enemy of the German people".

In May Trump's campaign committee produced a television ad lauding his first 100 days in office as an unprecedented "success" and labeling major television networks – CNN, MSNBC, ABC, CBS – and their correspondents as "fake news" for not reporting his "winning".

Once a Soviet citizen, I've been checking my surroundings. Am I living in cosmopolitan New York? Am I back in a homogeneous Moscow reading the Pravda headlines about the drummed-up victories of the communist state and the denunciations of the enemies who plot to take it down? In fact, when I was growing up in the 1970s, not even Pravda used such ominous language for Kremlin critics.

In the first half of the last century, the term *vragi naroda* – enemies of the people – applied to those who disagreed with the Bolshevik government on the issues ranging from the planned economy to atheism. They took their cue from the French revolutionaries of the 1790s whose Reign of Terror led to thousands being executed for "betraying" the newly founded First Republic.

Under Joseph Stalin being labelled an "enemy of the people" became even more dangerous because it resulted in immediate death or imprisonment in a labour camp. But after Nikita Khrushchev, my great-grandfather, denounced Stalin and his system of gulag camps in his 1956 speech to the Soviet Communist Party, the *vragi* formula fell out of use.

Trump, appearing less democratic than the Soviet autocrat Khrushchev, has found himself using the "enemies of the people" line, and joining the current pantheon of world rulers who share his anti-free-speech podium: Russia's Vladimir Putin, Turkey's Recep Erdogan and China's Xi Jinping.

Of course, in the USA journalists, including MSNBC's Andrea Mitchell and CNN's Wolf Blitzer, who Trump so blatantly labelled as "fake" in a recent commercial, can freely provide the real facts on the president's megalomaniacal narrative. Their lives are not in

BELOW: A demonstration in support of free press outside the offices of The New York Times

The free press guarantees that the state's menacing language should never turn into menacing actions

danger compared to those reporting from other places. And yet when Trump tweets or his ads attack the news, even if not as brutally as the Kremlin's Pravda once did, and with less deadly consequences, it can still amount to an attempt at state censorship. Political fear, after all, is not only about personal experience or individual threats, it is a condition of society. Threats shouted from the top, even without physical harm, restrict public debate and public policy. They reinforce →

COMMUNISM IN THE USA

Following news that a teacher in the USA is being investigated for communist links, **Kieran Etoria-King** looks at the history of communism in the country

1877: The Socialist Labor Party, the first socialist political party in the USA, is formed

1917: The USA is the first country officially to recognise Russia's new provisional government after Tsar Nicholas II abdicates. When the Bolshevik government takes over in the October Revolution, the USA refuses to recognise it

1919: The Communist Party USA is created

1920: In the first "Red Scare", between 3,000 and 10,000 immigrants are arrested and several hundred deported

1937: Just over 2,000 party members of the CPUSA and the party's youth league volunteer for the Lincoln Battalion to fight on the Republican side in the Spanish Civil War

1947: The House Committee on Un-American Activities, set up to search for communists, claims the film industry has been infiltrated and produces its Hollywood blacklist. More than 300 people are named and boycotted. They have to appear before the committee as "friendly" witnesses and incriminate others to have boycott lifted

1949: 11 CPUSA leaders are convicted of plotting to overthrow the government in the Foley Square trial. This leads to around 100 other CPUSA members being prosecuted, some just for being members of the party

1950: Senator Joe McCarthy orders a series of investigations and hearings to expose communists in the US federal government. The term McCarthyism is coined

1956: The New York Times publishes Russian leader Nikita Khrushchev's speech to the Communist Party Congress exposing evidence of Stalin's crimes, leading to falling membership in the CPUSA

1968: FBI director J. Edgar Hoover calls Marxist Black Panther Party, who internally promote Mao's Litte Red Book, "the greatest threat to the internal security of the country"

1989: The collapse of the Soviet Union creates a crisis of identity for the CPUSA

2017: The New York City Department of Education's Office of Special Investigations opens a case in March against a school principal, Jill Bloomberg. Bloomberg is accused of campaigning for the Progressive Labor Party, a Communist organisation, in contravention of education department policy

Kieran Etoria-King is editorial assistant at Index

→ social and political inequalities and create an atmosphere of mistrust and animosity between political parties and social groups.

In democratic societies, the free press guarantees that the state's menacing language should never turn into menacing actions against its people, as happened with Stalin's gulags. With Trump, who has more in common with Putin and Xi than with Canada's Justin Trudeau or Germany's Angela Merkel, we can no longer be so certain. ⊗

Nina Khrushcheva teaches international affairs at The New School in New York. She is the author of The Lost Khrushchev: A Journey into the Gulag of the Russian Mind

"This gripping account is a re-enactment of the Russian Revolution... His writing can be as passionate as that of the poets of the time... Miéville's own special effects are of a piece with them." - *Financial Times*

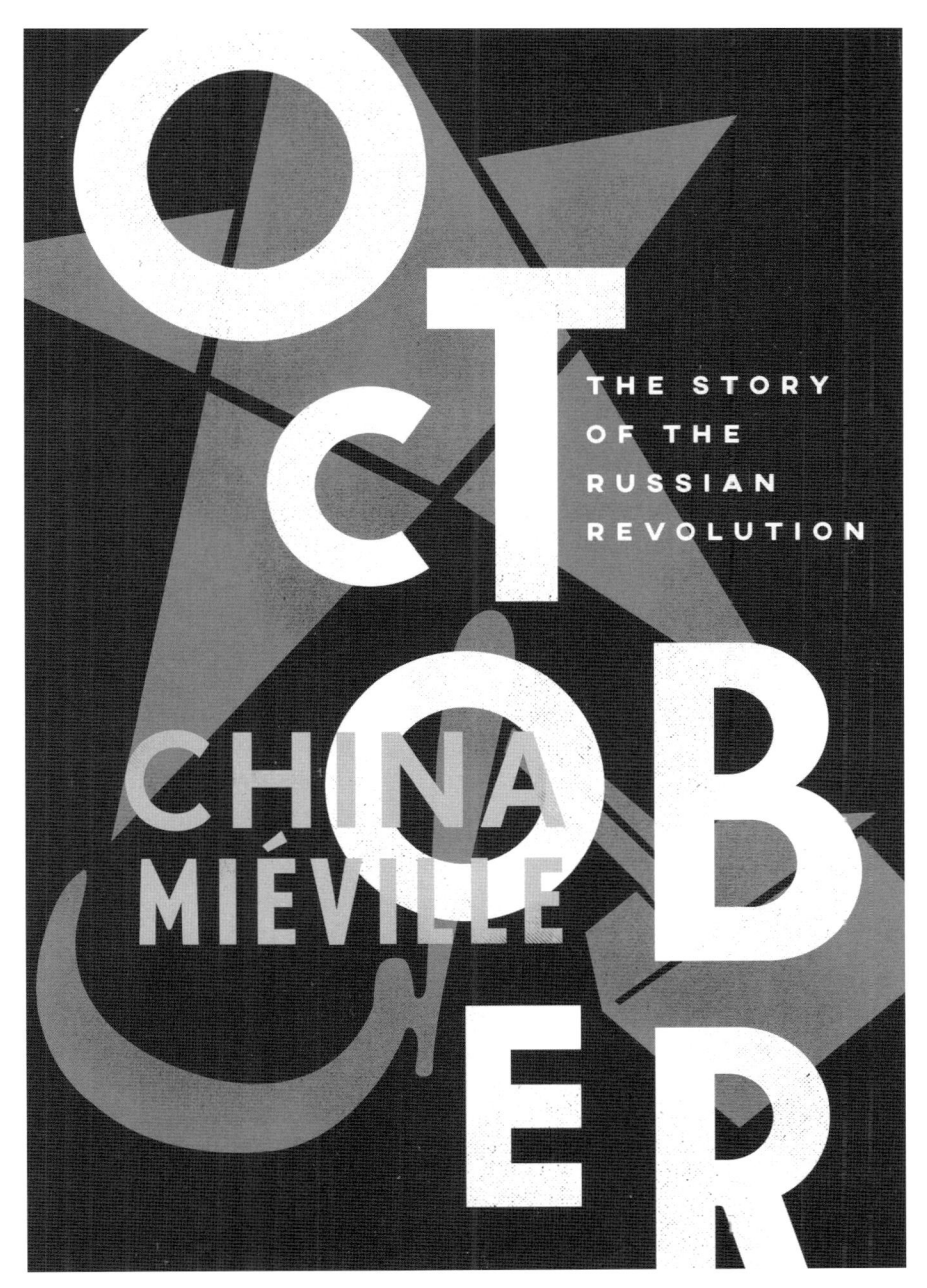

October: The Story of the Russian Revolution
by China Miéville

Hardback • May 2017 • £18.99 • 978 1 78478 277 1

versobooks.com
For regular updates on Verso titles and events see our Facebook page, Verso Books and follow us on twitter @VersoBooks
Available at all good bookshops and through our website.

VERSO

Airbrushing history

The way the 1917 Russian revolution can be remembered in China is an illustration of how stories of the past can be biased towards a view that the state approves, write historians **Jeffrey Wasserstrom** and **Yidi Wu**

CHINESE INTELLECTUALS LI Dazhao and Cao Dafu could not have had more different takes on Soviet Russia and it was these differences that led to the demise of one and the celebration of another. Unlike the Russian centenary, it is not easy today, with Mao's heirs still in power, to commemorate the 60th anniversary of a 1957 campaign that led to the purge of many intellectuals, including Cao.

So why is Li remembered and Cao forgotten? In The Victory of Bolshevism, an essay published in 1918 to mark the first anniversary of the October Revolution, Li wrote: "The red flag flies everywhere, the Soviets are established everywhere... Call it revolution entirely *à la Russe*... See the world of tomorrow: it assuredly will belong to the red flag!"

Li dreamed of a day when China would be blanketed with red flags, in the way that Russia already was. But by the 1950s, some people were insisting that following in Russia's footsteps, as China had, was the stuff of nightmares not dreams. In 1957, Cao wrote: "The Party central wants to do good things, but this isn't what happens. Socialist countries have a tower-like ruling system, with national issues decided by the Party and Party decisions made by one person... each a petty Stalin."

Li's Victory of Bolshevism appeared in Xin Qingnian (New Youth), an influential progressive periodical. It was a celebrated work. And today, because he co-founded the Chinese Communist Party in 1921, his name is widely known. It appears in the textbooks used in schools, as well as in newspapers, including official communist mouthpiece, People's Daily. There was even a play about him staged in Beijing's National Centre for the Performing Arts in 2012, called My Father Li Dazhao.

By contrast, Cao's text was never read widely and it was discovered buried deep in a book from the university that he worked at. The quotation was found in the People's University collection of rightist comments published by the school's socialist education department in 1958. Cao was recorded as an editor at the People's University Press. Those are the only details and nothing is mentioned of what became of him, an example of what can happen to people when they offer the wrong narrative on communist China. Cao is now largely forgotten, as the Communist Party has tried to eradicate the memories of those that were critical of the Soviet Union, and therefore by proxy critical of their own government.

And yet both Li and Cao operated at pivotal moments in China, moments that appeared full of promise when it came to free speech. For Li, many Chinese progressives circa 1917 were internationally minded, but also patriotic. They wanted to see China

CREDIT: Jason Lee/Reuters

become a country where people were freer and the government better able to stand up to bullying by Western powers and a rising Japan. In New Youth and other similar publications, they championed different imported creeds, from anarchism and non-Marxist forms of socialism to liberalism, as offering solutions to the problems plaguing their homeland.

After the Bolsheviks took power, a small number of people made the case for a new ideology: Marxism-Leninism. None did so with more gusto than Li, both in the essay quoted above and in other works, such as The New Epoch, which was published at the start of 1919. There he referred to people living "in dark China and in deadly silent Beijing" being able to see in Russia "the first glimmerings of the dawn lighting up the road to a new life".

The number of Chinese intellectuals embracing Bolshevism stayed low until the coming of the May 4th Movement, an enormously important series of 1919 protests, which began with a Beijing student march and culminated with a Shanghai general strike. It was triggered by anger at terms of the Treaty of Versailles that gave former German possessions in Shandong to Japan, rather than returning them to China. But when the authorities arrested students for taking to the streets, it also became a fight for freedom of expression and the right to protest as well. The fact that US President Woodrow Wilson supported Japanese claims over Chinese ones, after gaining supporters in China as a promoter of national "self-determination," left many May 4th activists looking for a new place to pin their hopes. Lenin's criticism of imperialism and the Soviet Union's repudiation of the tsarist government's past mistreatment of China, inspired some May 4th activists to form communist study societies, paving the way for the founding of the CCP.

When the People's Republic of China was founded in 1949, the Soviet Union became its closest ally and Stalin the foreign figure with whom Mao identified most closely. In 1957, the CCP celebrated the 40th →

BELOW: A boy sits in front of a portrait of Stalin in Nanjie village, Henan province

SHOOTING VIDEO STARS

China has moved far from its communist roots of celebrating the nation's have nots. Now it doesn't want you to see them, writes ROBERT FOYLE HUNWICK

Time magazine nominated "the Chinese worker" for Person of the Year in 2009. Eight years later, this anonymous figure remains invisible in mainstream Chinese media. Its exclusion explains how video-sharing and live-streaming app Kuaishou ("fast hand") has quietly become the fourth most popular app in China, while being largely ignored in favour of social media giants such as Weibo, a Chinese Twitter. But it's not being ignored anymore – a government crackdown is underway.

Kuaishou's content ranges from the bizarre to the controversial, such as pregnant teens and overweight children smoking. Its most newsworthy videos, including a challenge involving a power drill and a cob of corn that saw one user lose her hair and another his two front teeth, have sealed its unenviable reputation of being the Jackass of China, or worse, a stain on the nation's character.

The government is now taking steps to corral all live-streaming apps, of which Kuaishou is the biggest, cracking down on what the traditional-minded ministry of culture described as "vulgarity, obscenity and wrong life values". Among the many Kuaishou victims of the new regime: a glass-eating granny, a chilli oil-swigging food vendor, virtually all foreigners and, most famously, anyone eating bananas suggestively. Users have had accounts suspended without explanation or content deleted.

Some have been punished as a warning to others. Amateur pornographer Xue Liqiang was fined 100,000 yuan ($14,510) and sentenced to four years' prison last November for her role in a sex tape entitled Chengdu Foursome (pornography remains illegal in China).

Most Kuaishou users come from underdeveloped rural communities such as the frozen northeast, whose shuttered factories and desolate job prospects resemble the Rust Belt regions that make up modern Trump country. Their residents have been promised a Chinese Dream of individual prosperity by their president, Xi Jinping, but have little means of achieving it without money or connections. They are waitresses, taxi drivers, couriers, hairdressers, factory workers, the 674-million strong masses who comprise the country's service industries and keep the lights on.

To middle class critics, Kuaishou gives

→ anniversary of the October Revolution by holding a lavish banquet in Beijing. Mao, who only left China twice in his lifetime, also went to Moscow to participate in the Soviet celebration. A photograph in The People's Daily showed him standing beside Stalin's successor, Nikita Khrushchev, applauding.

By then, though, trouble was brewing below the surface. Mao was deeply disturbed when word came of Khrushchev's famous 1956 "secret speech" denouncing Stalin's personality cult. This sparked a fear in Mao, which would grow greater over time, that someday a Chinese counterpart to de-Stalinisation aimed at him would occur. He worried as well about other 1956 developments in the Soviet bloc, especially the Hungarian Revolution. For Mao, the protests in Hungary were unjustifiable disturbances and the sending of Soviet troops a legitimate move to ensure order. He was concerned about a Hungarian-type uprising challenging his rule, but he seemed confident that doing certain things, such as launching the Hundred Flowers Campaign, could prevent this.

During the Hundred Flowers Campaign, Mao called on people to voice their opinions

unwanted insight into a rarely seen reality, one that serves as an admonishment for how China's rushed development has left vast swathes of the interior undereducated, desperate and neglected. In a viral essay on social media site Weixin, writer Hou Qiming described a generation of socially immobile youth whose naive hopes of achieving overnight fame forced them into desperate acts of self-harm, producing "vulgar and crudely made" content in the name of entertainment.

But many Chinese are also sensitive about imagery that depicts the country in a "backward" light; Dolce & Gabbana was recently criticised for a global ad campaign that included Beijing taxi drivers and street vendors and was said to show the old, poor side of China.

Executives are moving to tame the medium too by manufacturing their own streaming stars, using algorithms to determine the most market-friendly faces, voices, even accents. In the end, censors may not need to kill the video star; the market can do it for them. ⊗

Robert Foyle Hunwick is a writer and media consultant based in Beijing. He is currently working on a book about vice and crime in China

it as an effort to allow the discontented to let off steam without taking to the streets. What seems clear now is that Mao did not expect such harsh criticisms to be voiced, though he was certainly ready to move against those who attacked him. Cao's forthright comments, especially the fact that he made it clear that he felt Mao himself was a "petty Stalin", led to his being purged during 1957's Anti-Rightist Campaign.

Many alongside Cao were punished for exercising their free speech in this burst of dissent. In 1957, the CCP, which traced its roots back to the protests of 1919, turned against those who spoke out much the way that the warlords had in the era of the May 4th Movement.

Mao's heirs remain in power. They would prefer that the sufferings of people like Cao be forgotten, and his writings as well, lest members of new generations view his criticisms of the CCP's "tower-like" system of rule too apt a description of how things continue to operate in the PRC.

Li and Cao operated at pivotal moments in China, moments that appeared full of promise when it came to free speech

freely, so that the CCP could improve the way it governed. People were encouraged to voice criticism of Mao and the Communist Party and this they did. Activists posted comments and criticisms on spaces known as "democracy walls". Cao wrote his critique of Communist Party structures in response to this command. Mao said that he wanted to "let a hundred flowers bloom and a hundred schools of thought contend" and many took him seriously.

Some view that campaign as a cynical trap, laid by Mao, to draw out and then punish secret critics of the CCP. Others see

Li died in 1927, long before his dream of painting China red became a reality. With an ambition for more freedoms, would Li have been content with what China became or would he have lamented it much like Cao did and had his name buried as a result? ⊗

Jeffrey Wasserstrom is chancellor's professor of history at UC Irvine and the author of Eight Juxtapositions: China through imperfect analogies from Mark Twain to Manchukuo

Yidi Wu is finishing her PhD at UC Irvine and is a contributor to 1943: China at the Crossroads

Being the big man

46(02): 46/48 | DOI: 10.1177/0306422017716019

Angola's long-ruling president has crafted a personality cult straight out of Stalin's playbook to promote his own style of propaganda and distract the nation from the news, writes **Rafael Marques de Morais**

TO DEFLECT ATTENTION from a growing chorus of disaffected citizens, President José Eduardo dos Santos, a Soviet-trained oil engineer who has been in power for 41 years, uses propaganda reminiscent of Russia's Stalinist period. This propaganda, built around the cult of the president, is in evidence as August approaches, when Angola will hold its third consecutive multiparty elections against a backdrop of economic crisis and state corruption.

Dos Santos' personality cult and the propaganda underpinning it have been long-term features of the regime's coercive relationship with society. They are what remains of its communist past. Inimical to freedom of expression, they are consistently deployed to subvert democratisation and constitutional rights.

The propaganda targets all age groups and spheres. In 2006, as a preventive measure to counter negative information that Angolan youth might see online, The People's Movement for the Liberation of Angola's (MPLA) Office for Citizenry and Civil Society disseminated a brochure to teach moral values to Angolan children. It was entitled Educated Child, Happy Family. It taught children that they must always respect Dos Santos "as the president of all Angolans, and the symbol of national unity".

The chilling manipulation of children's education is only one example of the extremes that the Soviet-educated Dos Santos' personality cult has reached. Recently, a member of the MPLA, António Luvualu de Carvalho, shocked Angolans with his claim that "the oxygen we breathe is also the gain of peace". Luvualu de Carvalho made the statement on the state-owned Angolan Public Television to dispel criticisms against Dos Santos. The idea that the very air Angolans breathe is a gift of the president is reminiscent of the infamous Avidenko's praise of Josef Stalin. It went:

"O great Stalin, O leader of the peoples,
Thou who broughtest man to birth.
Thou who fructifies the earth,
Thou who restorest to centuries,
Thou who makest bloom the spring ... "

That De Carvalho made such a statement was perhaps expected. He is an integral part of the MPLA's propaganda machine, representative of the significant investments made in promoting the regime's image. In 2015, he was appointed to the post of roving ambassador which, in effect, positioned him as the "propaganda tsar" who would deflect criticisms of the Angolan regime made abroad.

The manipulation of information is further evidenced in the current official narrative of Angola's tragic civil war, which entrenches Dos Santos' personality cult. Described as the "architect of peace", the president is credited with ending the war in 2002. The narrative thus ignores his cen-

OPPOSITE: People walk in front of a portrait of Dos Santos in Luanda, Angola. The poster reads "The Architect of Peace"

Anyone who dares to criticise him is branded as either ungrateful or an enemy of peace and stability

tral role in the perpetuation of the conflict, which raged in Angola from the time the MPLA seized power in 1975 following independence. Dos Santos came to power in 1979, after the death of the first president Agostinho Neto.

With Dos Santos having been put forward as the symbol of peace and stability, anyone who dares to criticise him is branded as either ungrateful or an enemy of peace and stability. These accusations are commonly used to discredit critical voices.

The development of Dos Santos' personality cult has met with some resistance. Although the MPLA had been labelled "Afro-Stalinist" in some Western academic literature, Stalin himself was the subject of internal condemnation by most MPLA members during its socialist period. But as noted by General Manuel de Carvalho →

CREDIT: Estelle Maussion/AFP/Getty Images

"Pakas", a former political commissar and member of the central committee of the MPLA, the promotion of a personality cult was done out of political expediency. "The need to end with factionalism within the MPLA, and coalesce around a leader, led to the copying of some of Stalin's practices in building the cult of personality to craft a symbol of unity," he told Index.

With the achievement of peace in 2002, after 27 years of civil war, the former ruling communists openly became capitalists but had to concede some liberties for the people. Back then the regime allowed more freedom of assembly, to discuss critical issues for instance. Nowadays, it is hard to get a room to hold a meeting on subjects they do not like, and anyone who dares to protest gets beaten up. The president's personality

> **The maintenance of ignorance is a powerful means through which the regime supresses potential critics**

cult, however, remains in place, underpinned by a state media that remains monolithic and populated by Avidenko-type sycophants.

The media landscape is mostly dominated by state-owned media. Angola only has one daily newspaper, the state-owned Jornal de Angola, also known as "the Pravda" for its rabid defence of the regime. The private media sector is dominated by outlets owned by ministers, generals and other high-ranking MPLA officials, thus making the internet the only forum for freedom of expression in the country.

The majority of Angolans, however, have no access to the internet and, arguably, beyond the capital most rely on the broadcasting media to stay informed. Isolated critics are picked off, co-opted, persecuted or disposed of as the need arises.

State media promotes ignorance in the country. The maintenance of ignorance is a powerful means through which the regime supresses potential critics. It ensures the security of those in power, who have abandoned what the academic Crawford Young identified as the essential commitments of the nationalisms that underpinned liberation in Africa: the tackling of poverty, ignorance and disease.

Nowhere is abandonment of the promises of independence more obvious than in some of the president's own public statements. Just four years ago, during Angola's economic oil boom, Dos Santos defended the plundering of states in Africa, especially in Angola, by their ruling elites as a right. He claimed that "the primitive accumulation of capital in western countries took place hundreds of years ago and at that state the rules of the game were different. The primitive accumulation of capital that is taking place today in Africa needs to be adequate to our reality".

Nevertheless, in the age of the internet, Dos Santos is losing control over the flow of information. His personality cult may yet find itself on shaky ground. De Carvalho's comments inspired a torrent of memes against him and about the air Angolans breathe. Humour has become a powerful tool of subversion, easily disseminated through everyday interactions.

With Dos Santos set to retire in September, the state media is frenetically building a personality cult around his anointed successor, the Soviet-educated João Lourenço. It is all about the derogation of "the others"– those not affiliated with the MPLA – as unpatriotic and unfit to run the country. The official line is that Lourenço, following on from the "architect of peace", is the "peace driver", further evidence of the ongoing use of propaganda in Angola's political landscape. ⊗

Rafael Marques de Morais is an author and investigative journalist from Angola. He won the Index on Censorship Freedom of Expression Award in 2015 for journalism

The big chill

Staged press conferences, tapped phone calls and restrictions on mixing with locals were some of the difficulties of reporting from Russia for a US newspaper during the Cold War, writes **Bernard Gwertzman**

IT WAS SOON after I arrived in Moscow in 1969 to become bureau chief for The New York Times that I was alerted to the reality of being a reporter there. I received a telephone call from Andrei Amalrik, whom I had known by reputation as a leading dissident. Amalrik had been friendly with Henry Kamm, my Times predecessor, and invited me and my wife to dinner at his apartment in the "upscale" Arbat section of Moscow. I kicked myself later for being so naive as to not realise that my phone was bugged.

When we arrived at his apartment door, a well-dressed gentleman greeted us. I first assumed Amalrik lived in a collective apartment, which was not uncommon in Moscow in those days. But Amalrik ran up and whispered "*obisk, obisk*". At first I did not know the words, but then I remembered reading them in dissident literature. They mean "search, search".

His apartment was being taken apart by a group of police agents. After being questioned as to why I was there, we left and were trailed home by agents. Amalrik was later convicted for defaming the Soviet Union and sent to a prison. He was released in 1975 and allowed to emigrate to western Europe.

I was never sure if the police or KGB were in his apartment that night because they knew I was coming or whether it was purely by coincidence. Nevertheless, after this incident I never let my guard down again. In my time in Moscow, we correspondents and diplomats all assumed that our apartments were bugged by the KGB. My wife and I developed a technique of never mentioning a Russian's name out loud. We had a full-time maid who was named Shura, and we jokingly used to refer to her as "Colonel Shura", because we assumed she was being questioned on a regular basis.

During my time there from 1969 to 1971 – one of 25 US journalists – I also had to endure tight restrictions that the Soviet authorities placed on me, my wife and other correspondents. We lived in an apartment compound at 12-24 Sadovo-Samotachnaya inhabited only by Western correspondents and diplomats. There was a 24-hour police guard at the entrance to keep out any Russians, other than those who had specific reasons to be there. In other words, we were told from the moment we arrived that the authorities did not want us to mingle with Russians. The building then and now is affectionately called "Sad Sam" by its dwellers.

While it was easier to report compared to the early years of the Soviet Union, when all copy from foreign correspondents had to first be scrutinised by a censor, there were still many obstacles. There were few press conferences and certainly no televised →

→ ones. I only attended one high-ranking press conference during my time. Prime Minister Alexei Kosygin held it on 4 May 1970 to attack President Richard Nixon for sending US troops into Cambodia. Instead, what was de rigueur was to cover a speech by Communist Party leader Leonid Brezhnev to other communists at a party conference. The speech might go on for four hours and produce little news.

There was one other press conference of note, though again it was not really about news. In March 1971, when the Soviet Union had launched a campaign to herald its close relations with Egypt and to establish a major presence in the Middle East, we foreign correspondents were invited to the ornate House of Friendship. Under glaring lights, 40 Soviet Jews – including Deputy Minister Veniamin Dymshits, the highest-ranking Jew in the government – were sitting on a raised platform in front of us. One by one, with

There were few press conferences and certainly no televised ones

varying degrees of enthusiasm, they pledged their loyalty to the Soviet Union and asserted their hatred for Israel, Zionism and the USA.

To garner information, a correspondent and his staff had to read the Soviet press closely and the multitude of journals published there. We learned that Pravda, the official newspaper of the Communist Party, liked to publish major policy articles late at night so that they would appear before Russian news agency Tass's ticker. The suspicion was that allowed the party enough time to change the official line if need be.

I also developed a fondness for weekly newspaper Literaturnaya Gazeta, which published sociological pieces about Russian life.

Otherwise we relied on dissidents' *samizdat* – self-published reports. These were usually typed, carbon copied and handed to foreign reporters. I met several times with Zhores Medvedev, a Soviet biologist who had been sent for some time to a mental hospital because his views contradicted official ideology. On one occasion he handed over rolls of 35 mm film. They contained information about secret meetings of the Communist Party. Several articles came out of the information in that film.

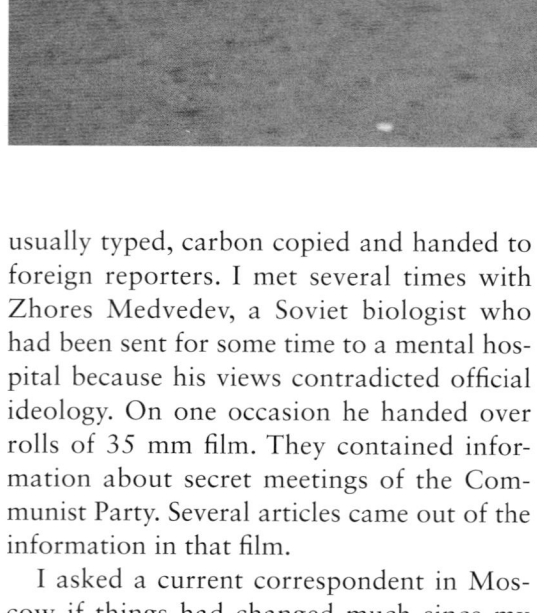

I asked a current correspondent in Moscow if things had changed much since my time there. He wished to remain anonymous and explained how there has been a significant drop-off in the number of Western correspondents in Moscow. He said this started when Dimitry Medvedev became president in 2008. Medvedev is now prime minister

SPECIAL REPORT

and accused by the current wave of Russian protestors of being corrupt.

Whereas the Sad Sam compound once housed dozens of Western correspondents, now there are just six or so. Papers no longer represented include The Baltimore Sun and The Los Angeles Times. The correspondent noted that "access to the government has gotten steadily worse along with the decay in political relations" between Russia and the USA. Correspondents can speak to the spokesman for the foreign ministry, "but any request to interview someone inside the ministry itself or in the Kremlin is usually ignored or refused". He said: "To find out what is going on you need to always be circulating around the edges, not just at conferences, but talking to newspaper editors, political consultants and others who do have contact with the Kremlin types. It is a series of rings and there are not a lot of people in that innermost ring around Putin, so real information from deep inside is hard."

The saving grace is that social media is very active, with all manner of debates unfolding on Facebook and VKontakte, the Russian equivalent. The internet and social media would have been a godsend when I was a correspondent in Moscow. ⊗

Bernard Gwertzman reported from Moscow between 1969 and 1971 for The New York Times. He revisited the country as foreign editor of The New York Times in 1994 and has been back on other visits

ABOVE: A man reads a newspaper in Moscow's Chekov Street, 1967

There's nothing new about fake news

While Americans might just be getting to grips with "fake news", Belarusians have been dealing with these kinds of tactics for years, writes **Andrei Aliaksandrau**

FICTIONALISING THE NEWS is not a recent development in Belarus. In April, a story ran across state TV channels and newspapers showing horrific photos of protesters holding Molotov cocktails and other weapons. The protesters, the reports said, were part of the White Legion, whose members allegedly wanted to ignite an uprising in Minsk similar to the Euromaidan protests that spread through Ukraine in 2013 and 2014, and contributed to the Crimean crisis.

Interestingly, the producers and reporters

of these films and articles were anonymous. There were no titles, no bylines at all and no evidence to suggest the White Legion, which used to exist, had operated on any level in the last few years. Interestingly, the police and the security forces would not answer any enquiries from journalists or from the public about the case.

The story, it turned out, was just made-up, packaged as news, a piece of twisted reality, broadcast to spread fear and panic within society. The message was: do not go out in the streets and protest. Those who do undermine peace and stability.

This is a typical tactic, and has been for years, in Belarus, where real news is suppressed and fake news flourishes. It is a tactic being used a lot at the moment, as 2017 has witnessed the most intense protests the country has seen in years, with a violent backlash from the government.

Under Soviet rule Belarus was quite prosperous. But when the USSR fell, Belarus went into economic decline. In the midst of economic and political turmoil, Alexander Lukashenko came to power. President Lukashenko retains his power 23 years later. This is largely due to his tight control of the media. Attacks against the free press, bloggers, independent writers and journalists have continually run alongside the activities of an extensive state propaganda machine.

News programmes on state-owned TV channels, and there are no national TV channels other than state-owned ones, follow a simple, yet persuasive pattern: here comes news about the president; here he comes greeting a foreign ambassador and making a speech about the special role Belarus plays in stability and peace in the world; here he comes meeting the minister of the interior making a statement about the importance of preserving stability and peace within the society; here he comes shouting at the cabinet of ministers that they have to do whatever it takes to follow his wise ideas in the interests of the people (not to mention peace and stability); here he comes visiting a factory in a small city talking to workers like a caring father, telling them he will provide for them.

After half an hour of this, there follows a kaleidoscope of images from the rest of the world: shells falling on Ukraine; bombs destroying a hospital in Syria; some weird president making some delirious statements across the ocean; a terrorist blowing up another city in Europe; refugees, floods, recessions, collapsing governments.

And then a story of happy children in a Belarusian kindergarten. Some more images of a peaceful country led by a wise leader that remains the last resort of happiness, the last island of stability in the violent world.

But there are other kinds of programmes on state TV. They are aired when the authorities feel the picture of "peace and sta-

The story, it turned out, was just made-up, packaged as news

bility" they broadcast contradicts the other reality, the one people see on the streets and at their work places, in grocery stores and on public transport, in hospitals and in schools. The one of life outside the matrix of state propaganda.

At the beginning of 2017, thousands of people across Belarus went into the streets to protest. The protests were triggered by the new presidential decree number three that fines people who cannot prove an official job or income. It has been dubbed the "social parasite" decree. There is an old Soviet term, *tuniejadcy*, which literally means parasite, and "parasitism" was considered a criminal offence in Soviet times, as everyone was expected to work to build "the utopian communist society". Here is a Belarusian innovation: instead of paying benefits to the unemployed, the government has decided to fine them.

OPPOSITE: Riot police detain a demonstrator during an unauthorised protest marking the 99th anniversary of the establishment of the Belarusian People's Republic

CREDIT: Viktor Drachev/Tass/PA Images

This decree was only a trigger. The real reason for the protests lies in the deep economic crisis gripping the country. Belarusian "stability" turns out to have been a coma. Our industrial-centred economy was inherited from Soviet times and has never been reformed. Reforms would have meant privatisation, changing laws to ensure guarantees to capital, the independence of the judiciary and a properly elected parliament, instead of one appointed by the president. All these steps, had they been taken, would have undermined the very core of the authoritarian regime.

Thus, the economy of the country has remained largely unchanged. For almost two decades, it was supported by cheap oil, gas and loans from Russia, which the Kremlin

> There is a video of him shouting "I am a journalist!" to uniformed thugs

could afford because of high oil prices and a need for a nearby ally. But today that relationship has cooled, in part because Belarus has opposed Russia's annexation of Crimea.

Economic difficulties have become noticeable to people, especially in small towns. Then came the "social parasite" tax, which acted as a trigger for protests. People took to the streets of Belarus for the first time since 2011, or even, in some small towns, since the 1990s.

The response was harsh. Hundreds of people were detained by the police, despite the completely peaceful manner of their protests. During events in Minsk in March 2017 the riot police used brutal force and arrested about a thousand people. Some were accidental passers-by. Some were journalists with valid credentials.

Aliaksandr Barazenka, a cameraman of Belsat TV channel, was detained during protests on 25 March 2017 in Minsk. There is a video of him shouting "I am a journalist!" to uniformed thugs, who grabbed him and dragged him into a police van. Later in court the riot police officers said Barazenka was swearing in public. The judge paid no attention to clear discrepancies in their accounts. Barazenka was sentenced to 15 days of administrative arrest and spent them in a detention centre on hunger strike.

There are many more similar examples of this during spring 2017. But these are the stories they never show on state TV.

There are still some forms of independent media in Belarus. There are still non-state newspapers and online publications that show what is going on. There are bloggers and social networks. In fact, when state media aired the staged scene with the Molotov cocktails, a video surfaced online that revealed there were no police or alleged criminals there, just a van and a bunch of state TV cameramen.

Stories of the journalist Barazenka and other detained protesters are being told. Sadly, though, the delirious and vicious reality of state TV prevails.

"The words of the media have been devalued. The authorities are not interested any more in what we know and think about them," wrote Viktar Martinovich, a bestselling Belarusian writer, in the Belarus Journal. "They do not need an audience anymore. They are on their own. They think they are powerful enough and they are eternal. And we lack words to prove they are wrong."

I believe we shall find the words. ⊗

Andrei Aliaksandrau is a journalist based in Minsk, Belarus. He is editor of the Belarus Journal

Help! I'm a Taiwanese communist

Michael Gold talks to communists in a nation that has been in conflict with China since 1949, and finds out whether they feel under pressure

WHEN MAO YI-YU, a self-declared communist, tells people of his political affiliation the reaction he gets usually ranges from disinterest to outright revulsion. Those who show genuine openness to the idea are few and far-between. Now 28 years old, he discovered communism in university. The understanding of the ideology among average Taiwanese people is extremely superficial.

"I start from base principles in discussions with friends about communism. I'll put forth an analysis of capitalism, where it goes wrong and how much it promotes the exploitation of labour and why communism is a better solution," he told Index.

He acknowledges that Taiwan is not likely to become a communist paradise anytime soon, but said he wants to inject more left-wing values into the debate.

Communism occupies a peculiar place in Taiwan. On the one hand, the island is locked in a perpetual stare-down with a powerful, nominally communist China that considers it a part of its territory. Tensions show no signs of lessening, as the fiasco over Trump's December phone call with Taiwanese president Tsai Ing-wen showed, as well as the recent detention in China of Lee Ming-che, a Taiwanese activist. On the other hand, it is a liberal democracy in which no political view, including that of the far left-wing, is off-limits. Yet communism is particularly fraught. Mention the word to any Taiwanese and the association with China is likely to colour his or her impression. Being open about being communist is not always easy, though the tide has turned a bit in recent years as Mao can testify.

Taiwan's unique relationship with China has pushed the island's political debate away from the conventional left-right divide of the West. Rather, Taiwan's binary is far starker: unification with China or independence. Within both of these camps, a rainbow of views exists regarding the role of the state in the economy and the redistribution of wealth. Neither of Taiwan's two main parties, the Kuomintang (KMT) and Democratic Progressive Party, adheres to a platform that neatly encompasses either side.

People like Mao Yi-Yu were not always able to hold such views openly. Throughout much of its modern history, communism →

ABOVE: Students look at a monument in Taipei in 2016 to the victims of Taiwan's White Terror purge, when thousands were tortured and killed for being "anti-government" in the 1950s and 1960s

→ was subject to a violent crackdown by the KMT, which ruled Taiwan as a dictatorship after suffering defeat in a civil war on the mainland by Mao Zedong's communists in 1949. Though the island boasted a small communist movement in the 1920s and 1930s, anyone with a whiff of Marxist thought was harshly persecuted in the 1950s and 1960s, during a period known as the White Terror. The campaign targeted anyone thought to oppose the KMT's rule. During the White Terror, the KMT conducted numerous executions for alleged political resistance (estimates extend to tens of thousands), with many arrests and subsequent executions occurring either publicly or in the middle of the night. Those who weren't executed were imprisoned and some subjected to "psychological therapies, re-education and forced composition of confessional letters".

Communists comprised a significant share of those purged, Bo Tedards, former director of Amnesty International's Taiwan chapter, told Index. He notes that defections to the communist party contributed to the KMT's loss during the Chinese Civil War, and that the KMT had reason to be paranoid about infiltration by refugees from the mainland. Yet the KMT used the threat of communist insurrection as a pretext for a broader societal crackdown and continues to cite it as justification for its abuses, said Tedards, who maintains that this so-called threat was minimal.

At the end of last year civic groups held simulated trials of White Terror-era anti-communist cases, examining them strictly based on the Republic of China constitution, which the KMT brought to Taiwan. It found the statutes invoked at the time to justify the convictions of alleged communists to be unconstitutional.

The KMT's anti-communist zeal extended even beyond Taiwan's shores. In an incident

CREDIT: Sam Yeh/AFP/Getty Images

from 1970, two ethnic Chinese brothers were deported from the Philippines, where they were born, to Taiwan, where they stood trial for publishing a pro-communist newspaper in Manila. They were eventually found guilty and sentenced to prison.

Since the island democratised in the late 1980s, restrictions against promoting communism have been relaxed, and in 2008 the island's courts ruled such restrictions unconstitutional. Parties at the left end of the spectrum have sprung up since, including numerous with the word "communist" in the title. The Taiwan People's Communist Party, for example, was established in February by a former KMT official with the aim of promoting economic socialism and peace across the Taiwan Strait.

Another left-wing group, the Taiwan Communist Party, came into existence the same year as the high court decision striking down the ban. In an interview with Index, its founder, Wang Laoyang, railed against inequality, though the party disavows seizure of wealth and promotes "democracy" and "human rights" on its Facebook page. Wang says he agrees with the notion of joining China, via a process "of getting to know each other and making friends", and details exchanges he's had with Chinese Communist Party officials. He believes that greater interaction could instigate reform within China and make it more democratic.

Individual communists like Mao, those who genuinely believe in its principles, are few and far between. There are many reasons for this: chief among them are the link with China and the sense that communism simply does not work as a national organising principle.

Fear of persecution, however, does not rank on that list these days. Largely due to their decades of repression and crackdown, the Taiwanese have cultivated a level of political openness and tolerance rare in Asia. Political groups from across the spectrum all enjoy their niche. Election season commonly sees caravans of banner-draped vans parading the streets, trumpeting (literally) their messages into the air. Most Taiwanese value their democracy too much to allow any form of repression to seep back into society.

Despite communism's poor reputation, Yi-Yu, for one, believes that "real communism is totally democratic" and that the "soft" promotion he engages in – attending labour-rights meetings, publishing essays espousing his views – can help people realise that. But, as is the case in most centre-right Western nations, "nobody is interested in this".

Communism inevitably carries connotations of reunification and political watchers do not foresee much success for efforts to infuse far left-wing views into Taiwan's political realm. Bruce Jacobs, director of the Taiwan Research Unit at Australia's Monash

Those not executed were imprisoned or subjected to psychological 'therapies'

University, said simply that "there's no market for it" and that the poor support for reunification – only 18.5% in a poll taken last year – makes communism particularly unpopular.

Ironically, the KMT now advocates for greater economic co-operation with so-called communist China. Yet China's iron-fisted repression of democracy is anathema to most Taiwanese, who last year voted the KMT out of office after eight years in power, ushering in the more pro-independence DPP.

Though Taiwan has very little stomach for communism, either in the classical Marxist or modern Chinese sense, its people are at least now capable of discussing it.

Michael Gold is an editor at The Economist Intelligence Unit in Hong Kong. He was previously a reporter for Reuters in Taipei

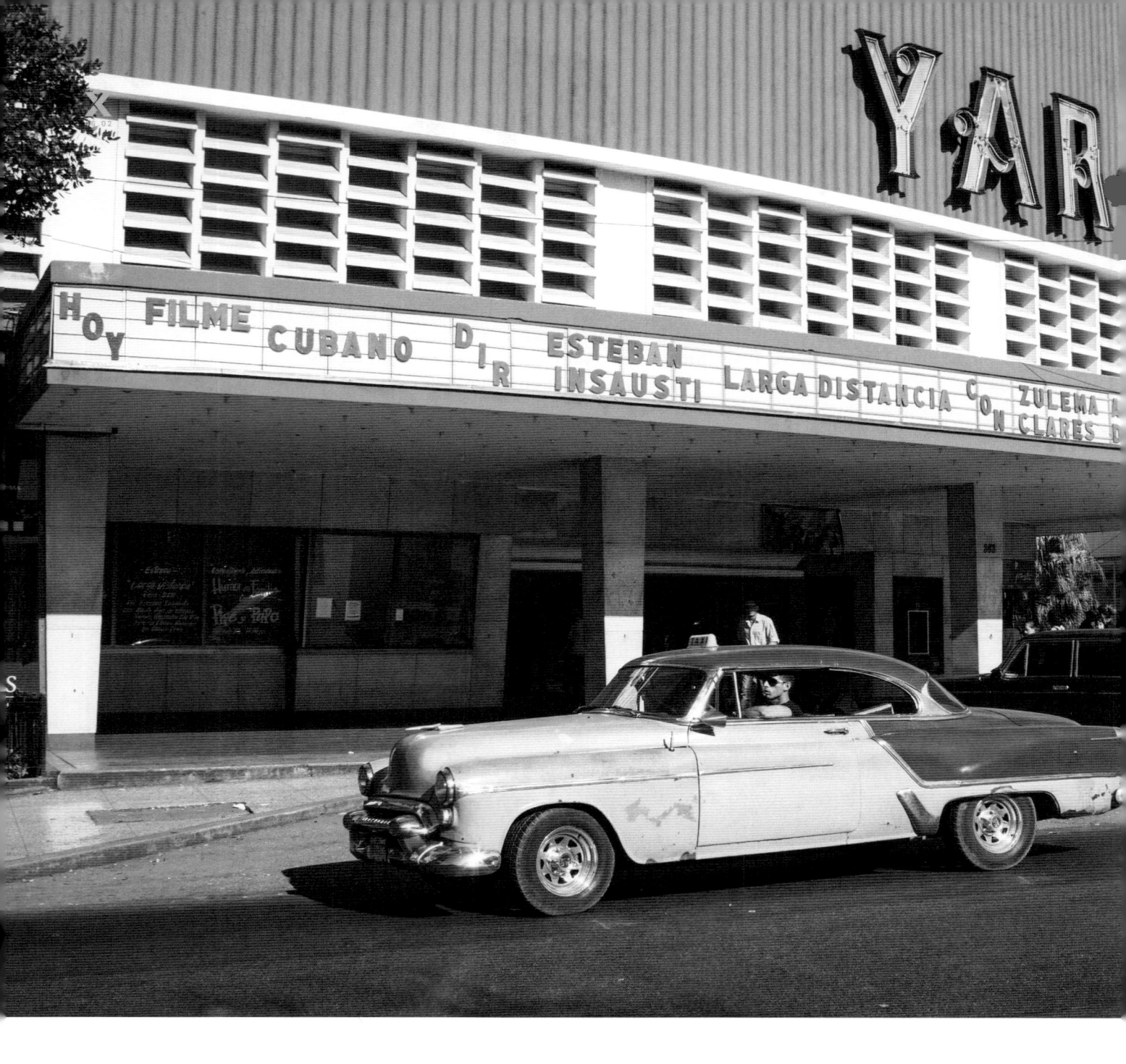

Shot in Havana

The ideals of the 1917 Russian Revolution arrived somewhat late in Cuba, but when Fidel Castro seized power in 1959, they took root, not only in politics but in cinema. Leading Cuban film maker **Luis Lago Diaz** talks to **Jan Fox** about the past and his hopes for a new filmmaking era

SPECIAL REPORT

LEFT: The famous Yara cinema in Havana, Cuba, which hosts the annual International Festival of New Latin American Cinema

CREDIT: Franck Vervial/Flickr

"AS FAR AS the government is concerned I am non-existent right now," Cuban filmmaker Luis Lago Diaz told Index. "They don't recognise independent producers because all filmmaking must go through the film institute channels and I have to do the same."

Diaz, 49, runs his own production company Shoot Cuba. He learned his craft as a young man at the state controlled Cuban Film Institute (ICAIC), working on scores of films including the landmark movie Strawberry and Chocolate, which was the first Cuban film to be recognised at the Oscars. He struck out on his own as an independent producer in 2001.

But it has not been easy. The state still wields a lot of power over the film industry, a hangover from when the Soviet Union was at its height, and Castro's Cuba was an outpost of communism in the Caribbean.

And yet, for the first time in decades said Diaz, ordinary Cubans are getting more connected to the wider world. "Two or three years ago, we had no internet – only in some government offices," he said. "Now Wi-Fi is in some hotels and there are some public Wi-Fi hotspots in Havana, though in the street, not yet in cafes. We are getting more US films too, though many are pirate versions but shown in cinemas – a movie ticket is about $2 Cuban – around 16 cents US."

And that has led many young Cuban filmmakers, including himself, to try and get the law changed so that independent producers and filmmakers, who are not part of the state machine, are given official recognition.

"We are in the digital era now so it's getting harder for the government to control everything – I can make a film on my cellphone so why do I have to do everything through the government? Of course, many of the younger filmmakers don't know about the old times. I'm the guy in the middle, who knows the old times and the new."

In 1959, after the revolution, when the Cuban Film Institute was first set up under government auspices, the state censors were in total control of filmmaking. The melodramas of previous Cuban cinema were replaced by documentaries and films, which all supported revolutionary ideals.

Despite what would seem to be a curtailment of freedom of expression, this post-revolutionary period of filmmaking was known as the golden age in Cuba because it produced so many films which were much higher quality than before.

"I never thought too much about censorship," said Diaz who was born eight →

→ years after the revolution. "You just accepted it if you wanted to make films. If you opposed the censor you might not be able to make another film or if you did, it wouldn't get released or they might release it for one showing at 3pm in a town in the middle of nowhere just to say they'd allowed it to be released. The president of the film institute, Alfredo Guevara, [who died in 2013] often fought the censors. He was a founder member of ICAIC, a revolutionary who fought with Fidel, a brave man. He helped the film makers a lot.

"He would get filmmakers to work around the problem, through careful editing, to keep the essence of the film but avoid the censor. That's what happened with Strawberry and Chocolate, which had gay characters and that was not permitted, though even outside Cuba it was difficult to make a film about gays then," Diaz pointed out.

Diaz can pinpoint the exact moment his love affair with film began. Working in his first job as a production driver at the film institute, the cameraman he was ferrying around set up a shot of a billboard that read: "To revolution and socialism today we owe everything we are".

Diaz recalled: "Public transport in Cuba is terrible and so we waited until the worst camel bus [the equivalent of a bendy bus] came by. People were packed in like sardines, some hanging out the windows or clinging onto the outside and as this monster rolled past the sign, he shot it. For me, it was brilliance and I realised at that moment what an image can do and I fell in love with film making."

Castro also recognised the power of the moving image. "Fidel was a fan of films and was very knowledgeable about them. My former boss Miguel Mendoza was a producer and he would screen films for Fidel at ICAIC at 3am almost every day so that he could see them and check their quality," said Diaz.

From driving cast and crew around, Diaz moved on to learning about, and making, films in what he calls a dream apprenticeship.

"They gave me projects non-stop – it was crazy," he said. "I was making five or six films a year and I was very young. Later, in Spain, they accused me of lying about my CV because I had so many credits on it. The Film Institute gave me a tremendous opportunity to learn my craft and work far more than I would have done had I been somewhere like Los Angeles."

He said: "With regard to censorship, you have to remember that Cuba was like a Russian child and a child sometimes gets a slap on the wrist. Many good and bad things came out of this relationship. It may be hard to understand today, because now things are bad economically, but I've spoken to many people who tell me how much worse things were before the revolution. In my own family, there were seven people living in one room and many Cubans were starving.

"But like a child, we were very dependent on our parent and when the Soviet Union collapsed, it was a bad time because we lost all that support and funding. Now we had to grow up and be independent."

One area that was dramatically affected by this political divorce was filmmaking, and the new opportunities for working with film companies from all over the world that damaged Cuban cinema as an art form, according to Diaz.

"The film institute had no money to spend on film so started to encourage co-productions with international filmmakers. For me this was the worst moment in the history of Cuban film because you had, say, a French-Spanish co-production and they

> **With regard to censorship, you have to remember that Cuba was like a Russian child**

wanted to make something more commercial. The Cuban government just wanted to make pro-revolutionary films but these co-productions were about making a cliché of Cuba – Cuban music, people dancing in the streets, drinking rum, provocative women – which to me was worse. From 1989 to now everything is bad," said Diaz. "Artistically, I am more proud of my revolutionary years of filmmaking than now."

Aesthetics aside, Diaz's own career has flourished and he is a popular go-to for foreign filmmakers shooting in Cuba, facilitating everything from permits to catering, locations to crew. But it's his skill in making things work where people are used to "making do" that most find invaluable.

"My mother is a big communist who changed her dream of studying physics to be an agronomist because Castro said we needed agronomists. I agree with her on a lot of things and I want to show the world the good side of Cuba. I am an ambassador of Cuba. I have to explain that if you want to make films here, there are certain things you can't do. It does get hard when I try to make filmmakers understand why you can't put a corrupt cop or a prostitute in a script. They say 'but it's only fiction' and I say, you still can't do it but make some changes and you can still have your film. It's all about working within the system and I try to be transparent about that," said Diaz.

Diaz walks a diplomatic tightrope, dealing on one hand with international filmmakers eager to shoot in Cuba, and Cuban government officials who must still be seen to toe the party line.

He misses the old days of a film institute that made films with passion and love of craft, as well as the now legendary original members like Miguel Mendoza, Alfredo Guevara and Tomas Gutierrez Alea. It may be true that films had a political message back then, but these days, Diaz believes, the institute's emphasis is more on politics and bureaucracy than film. "It's so sad. I want to protect the memories of the original film institute," said Diaz.

LEFT: Cuban filmmaker Luis Lago Diaz

Nothing, though, in Cuba is simple. Diaz remembers growing up watching Russian cartoons and listening to endless talks by Castro in Revolution Square: "He would talk for four to six hours and we had to stand up the whole time," said Diaz. Yet the young Diaz was also secretly listening to "subversive" banned rock music under the bedclothes on an old FM radio.

And last year Diaz was among the massive crowd who enjoyed a free Rolling Stones open air concert in Havana, the first-ever rock concert on the island. Diaz recalled: "It was really amazing. Obama visited the same week. Such incredible change. Cubans are excited about the new relations with the US – you need a change after 56 years. But it's happening very fast and in Cuba we want to keep our integrity and not change because the US dictates terms to us."

Meanwhile, Diaz will continue to navigate between the old and the new order, while trying always to protect the essence of the country he loves through a changing lens.

Jan Fox is a writer and actor based in Los Angeles and is a contributing editor to Index on Censorship magazine

Global View

The tussle to ensure essential liberty is not eroded by catch-all "national security" measures is ongoing, argues **Jodie Ginsberg**

GERMANS GO TO the polls in September in an election that is likely, once again, to see security concerns pitted against civil liberties. As with so many elections worldwide in recent years, it is a fight that should give free expression campaigners renewed cause for concern.

Since 9/11, liberal democracies have increasingly implemented laws in the name of protecting the population against the threat of terrorism, but which have simultaneously undermined the rights of all citizens. From the Patriot Act, passed just 45 days after the attacks on the Twin Towers in New York in 2001, and which vastly expanded the ability of the US government to spy on ordinary citizens, to the recently approved Investigatory Powers Act in the UK, governments worldwide are engaged in a seemingly never-ending expansion of state power.

As is evidenced in recent proposals by the UK Law Commission, and in the conversation surrounding the UK general election after the London and Manchester attacks, security, rather than the protection of fundamental values and freedoms, is rapidly becoming the global goal. The Law Commission, which undertook a review of the country's outmoded spying laws, suggested that the current law, which protects the "safety or interests of the state", should be replaced with the term "national security".

Governments justify these fresh incursions into the lives of law-abiding individuals by arguing there are new terrorist threats, and, in particular, that the internet is being used to spread and enable terrorism.

This is where the nebulous formulation "national security" becomes highly problematic, as the definition of what constitutes a threat to such security grows ever wider.

Recent attempts by governments to deal with content online are a case in point.

Take the example of Pakistan's Prevention of Electronic Crimes Act, passed last year as part of a 20-point National Action Plan against terrorism that Prime Minister Nawaz Sharif announced, after an attack on a school in Peshawar left 141 people dead.

The cyber crimes bill is meant to limit the amount of hate speech online and protect internet users against malicious cybercrimes. A lack of clarity about what speech is, and is not, protected means that government critics and other dissenters have been silenced as a result of the law; few effective moves have yet been made against real malicious threats. For example, as former Index on Censorship Freedom of Expression Award winners Bolo Bhi pointed out, the Khabaristan Times, a satirical media organisation, was recently blocked online under Section 38 of PECA, which allows the government to remove and censor any "objectionable content".

GLOBAL VIEW

Criminalisation of political criticism and expression and a tightening environment for journalists are all hallmarks of attempts by government to tackle extremism through measures aimed at restricting speech in the name of national security.

In Turkey, hundreds of journalists have been arrested and jailed in the wake of the failed 2016 coup, many of them because of reporting that is critical of the government, but it has also been alleged that they have damaged the "security of the state". World-renowned cartoonist Musa Kart, known for his satirical lampooning of President Recep Tayyip Erdogan, is one of those currently detained and faces 29 years in jail if convicted.

In the USA, as our recent report on US media freedom showed (see p. 112), many journalists have found themselves detained at the US border and asked to hand over equipment and notes, threatening the anonymity and safety of sources – a key tenet of a free press. Searches of all travellers' phones by border agents grew an astonishing five-fold in 2016. In February 2017 alone, some 5,000 devices were searched, as many as in all of 2015.

Journalists (and indeed any US citizen) can legally have their phones and electronic equipment searched at the border without customs officers or Homeland Security officials having to prove any suspicion of wrongdoing. In one incident, Le Monde journalist Kim Badawi was held at Miami International Airport for 10 hours and questioned by Customs and Border Protection agents about his passport stamps for Middle Eastern countries, his political views and religious affiliation. His baggage was searched and he was forced to surrender the password of his phone so agents could go through his contacts, photos and messages, including confidential ones from Syrian refugees.

Increasingly, governments are also devolving responsibility for determining what constitutes unacceptable content to private companies.

Draft law approved by the German cabinet in April, for example, threatens fines on companies that fail to take down content that might contravene some 24 current provisions of the German Criminal Code, including offences as varied as "defamation of the state and its symbols", "anti-constitutional defamation of constitutional organs" and "defamation of religions, religious and ideological associations".

The measure effectively outsources decisions on the balance between freedom of expression and other legally protected rights to private companies and so threatens open and democratic discourse at the heart of one of the world's largest, most stable democracies.

In February 2017 alone, some 5,000 devices were searched, as many as in all of 2015

The idea that the threats we face are in some way more acute than those that have gone before – and therefore necessitate a restriction of hard-won freedoms – is not new.

"Those who would give up essential liberty to purchase a little temporary safety deserve neither liberty nor safety," argued US founding father Benjamin Franklin, showing the conflict goes back centuries.

Asked what he felt could most usefully be done to protect journalists in the current climate, Stefan Stojanovic, editor of Slovenian investigative news organisation KRIK, said he would reverse the tendency to prioritise national security over civil liberty.

Franklin would have agreed. ⊗

Jodie Ginsberg is the CEO of the Index on Censorship. She tweets @jodieginsberg

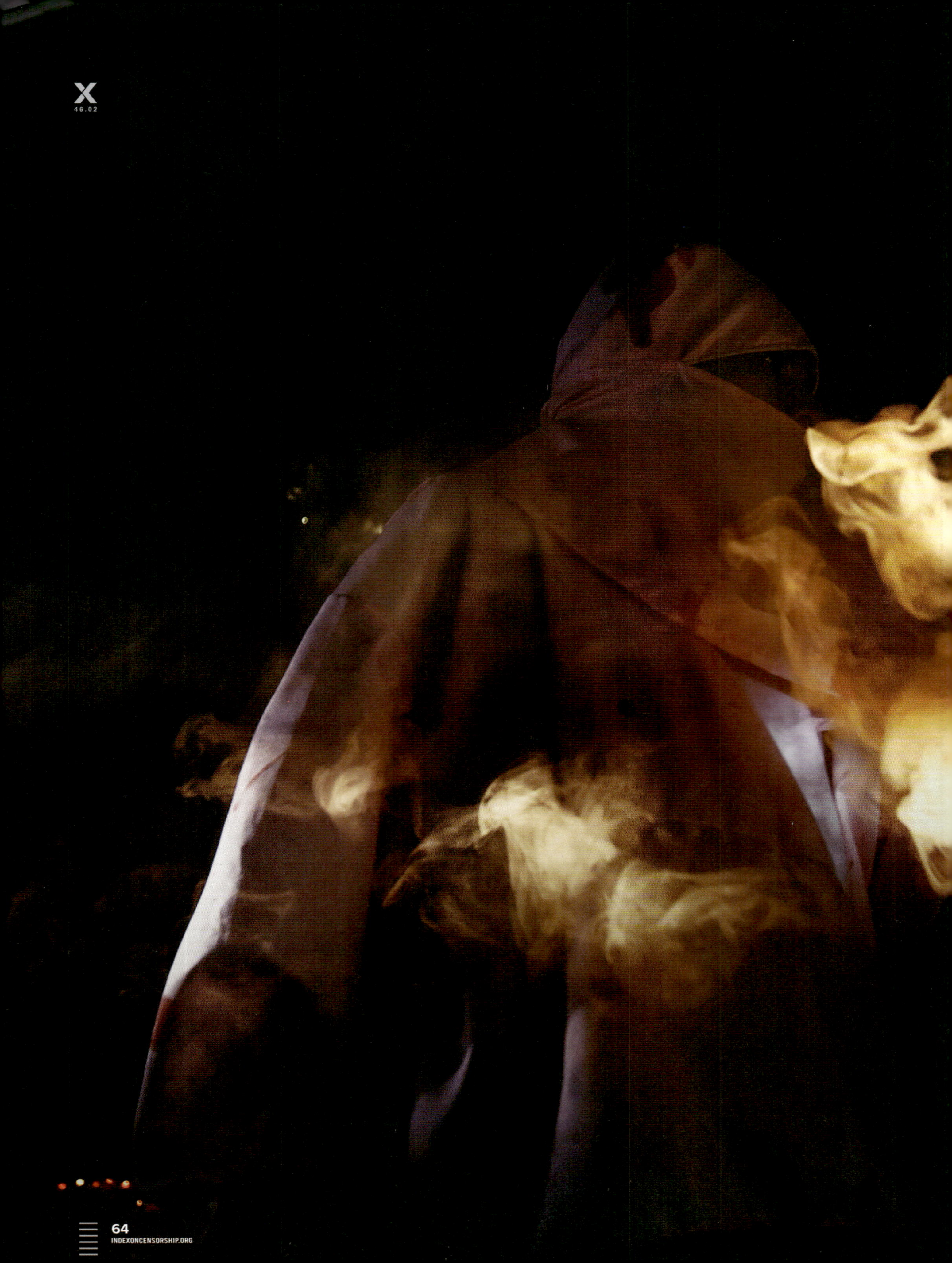

IN FOCUS

IN THIS SECTION

Provoking the president
RAYMOND JOSEPH **66**
South African cartoonist Zapiro on Zuma and the challenges ahead

Yemen: "Nobody is listening to us"
LAURA SILVIA BATTAGLIA **70**
A Yemeni journalist on threats to reporters in the country

Novel lines
JEMIMAH STEINFELD **73**
An interview with Margaret Atwood on commemorating free speech heroes

No country for free speech?
DANIEL LEISEGANG **76**
As Germany debates fake news and prepares for an election, free speech is increasingly under threat

Read all about it
JULIA FARRINGTON **79**
Ten years after its launch, Somalilanc's book festival opens up access to reading matter

See no evil **82**
A Chechen journalist on the dangers of writing about anything beyond flattering the president

No laughing matter
SILVIA NORTES **85**
A spate of prosecutions against comedians in Spain

Cementing dissatisfaction
ELIZA VITRI HANDAYANI **87**
Indonesians are experimenting with creative forms of protest including making casts of their feet

---

MAIN: An activist from the group Chok3 performs during a protest against reported violence directed at the gay community in Chechnya, outside the Russian embassy in Mexico City in April 2017

CREDIT: Carlos Jasso/Reuters

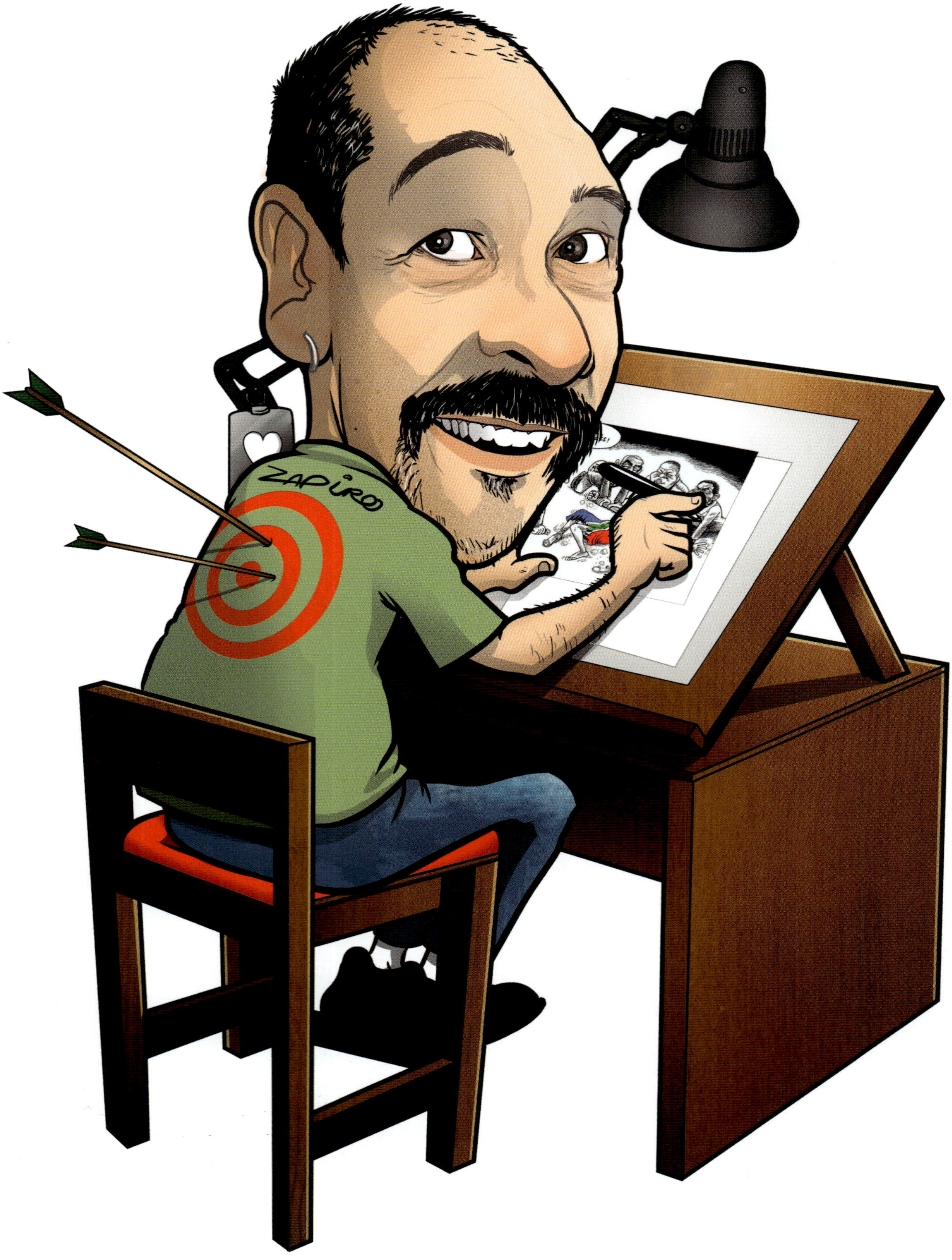
ZAPIRO

Provoking the president

In an exclusive interview, legendary South African cartoonist **Zapiro** talks to **Raymond Joseph** about being sued for millions by Jacob Zuma, fighting for "Lady Press Freedom" and death threats

YOUNGER CARTOONISTS ARE struggling with the role of their work and fears of causing offence, said Jonathan Shapiro, who draws under the pen name Zapiro, in an extensive interview with Index on Censorship.

Political correctness was increasingly forcing them to second guess how their work might be interpreted, argued Shapiro, who has held art shows in London, Frankfurt and New York, as well as across South Africa.

In his studio in Oranjezicht, a Cape Town suburb on the slopes of Table Mountain, the cartoonist outlines his fears for the future. Behind him, on bookshelves, are a set of mini collectable figurines of some of his cartoon characters, including Archbishop Desmond Tutu and Nelson Mandela.

"I have the stomach for the fight. But I see the discussions among younger cartoonists and they worry. Some are quite young and haven't figured out what is going to offend people," he said.

"People are scared of fanatics. But political correctness also plays a role and they fear even minor things. This has led to increased self-censorship by cartoonists because they are increasingly worried about sensitivities and the fear of causing offence," said the veteran cartoonist, who has drawn for the Cape Argus, Cape Times and Mail & Guardian.

With a dark history of oppression and censorship under apartheid, there is increasingly narrow space for robust debate in South Africa today. Charges of racism often stifle, or sometimes replace, debate and as a cartoonist, Zapiro is often the target of people offended by his cartoons.

That is in spite of his long history as an activist and his opposition to oppression and racism that goes back to his earliest days as a cartoonist in the early 1980s, when his work first appeared in the alternative press. He worked tirelessly to produce posters and pamphlets for anti-apartheid organisations and campaigns. This led to him being arrested and harassed by the feared special branch, which hunted down opponents of the apartheid government. It is a part of his history that many don't know about, while others choose to ignore it.

The latest controversy swirling around Zapiro is centred on his revisiting of a 2008 cartoon that showed powerful members of government and the ruling ANC holding down Lady Justice, as President Jacob Zuma prepares to rape her. In the 2017 cartoon, →

→ Zapiro drew the president zipping up his flies as Lady Justice, draped in the South African flag, is held down, while a member of a powerful family accused of state capture to get lucrative tenders with Zuma's help, prepares to have a turn raping her. He said he has no regrets about returning to the rape of South Africa as a theme.

He was sued for seven million rand ($528,163) by Zuma after the first cartoon and the case dragged on for four years until the president dropped it the day before it was due to be heard in court. Zuma had also earlier sued Zapiro for a series of three cartoons dealing with rape charges the president had faced, and which he had been acquitted of, before coming into office. The action against Zapiro dragged on for six years before it was also withdrawn.

On the first rape cartoon that caused a huge outcry, Zapiro said: "It was the most powerful thing I could have done and I don't regret it at all, or for revisiting it. I did always have more of a concern about how women would see it than anything else. I certainly wasn't concerned at all about how the targets would see it. The overarching reason for the cartoon was that Zuma, with the help

Cartoonists do get to occupy that jester space where you can sometimes say things using hyperbole and hypothetical stuff

of his allies, was bullying and threatening the judiciary to try and get the corruption charges lifted so he could become ANC president and then president of South Africa. It was as simple as that. He wanted, and got, a political solution dressed up as a legal one."

Never a stranger to controversy, his publisher ran into a bid to ban his cartoon strip of the Prophet Mohammed for South Africa's Mail & Guardian in 2010. They didn't back down, winning a last-minute court decision. Last year, Zapiro said his depiction of the National Prosecuting Authority boss as a monkey dancing to Zuma as an organ grinder was a mistake, and apologised.

"Cartoonists and satirists and columnists who are prepared to be irreverent or to push the boundaries are not the source of the real problem in society," said Zapiro.

"It is coming from a source people are not prepared to admit to; people who spend their lives waiting to be offended. Some of those people have authority and some are part of fanatical groups or attach themselves to fanatical groups. But to somehow cast the cartoonist or satirist as the provoker of that sort of violence when we are actually provokers of thought is utterly ridiculous."

Zapiro said he felt that with social media, some people were waiting to be offended and some were living in echo chambers hearing just themselves. This got amplified onto a bigger stage where even things used ironically or used to criticise others were then pounced on, twisted and convoluted, in order to have everyone conform to multiple banal sets of canards. "Different people have different things they are politically correct about. But this becomes a minefield when all of these people assert their beliefs. This is very difficult to deal with and the nuance gets lost in a cartoon."

Zapiro is aware of how political correctness could affect his work if he doesn't guard against it. "I try to differentiate between self-censorship and emotional intelligence and I now ask myself where the negative stuff will come out of a cartoon and overpower the positive aspects. In the case of the latest rape cartoon there has been a lot of negative response, but I also believe it will stand the test of time and it was worth doing."

He has received numerous death threats as a result of his cartoons, some of which he took very seriously. "I have had lots of death threats and I've also had calls in the middle of the night with threats, telling me they know where my children go to school."

LEFT: In this cartoon on the state of press freedom, Zapiro depicts the media attempting to expose government corruption

In the latest incident, in April, a court heard that Zapiro was included on a hit list compiled by twin brothers Brandon-Lee and Tony-Lee Thulsie, who are accused of planning acts of terror against US, British, Russian and Jewish targets in South Africa.

"People are losing sight of an idea that has been very important over the past few decades that you have no right not to be offended," he said. "The violence and the real transgression is coming from people who take their religious and other beliefs so seriously and are so fragile in their beliefs set that they can't tolerate anyone else not having the same view as them. It also comes from authoritarian regimes," he said.

Do cartoonists enjoy a privileged position in society, I asked. On the one hand, he said, cartoonists do not have any more rights than any other citizen has. "But on the other hand, by convention in a democracy, cartoonists do get to occupy that jester space where you can sometimes say things using hyperbole and hypothetical stuff, which can be so extreme as to seem as if you have more rights than other people.

"In other words freedom of expression allows one to be so startling and outrageous and potentially startling that it gives you that rarified position of being untouchable. Speech that should be acted against is that which incites hurt or killing, but that is not what cartoonists are doing. We provoke thought, even if that thought is pretty outrageous. Others can do it too. We just occupy a space where you can really push the boundaries."

Raymond Joseph is a former editor of Big Issue South Africa and regional editor of South Africa's Sunday Times. He is based in Cape Town and tweets @rayjoe

Yemen: "Nobody is listening to us"

Yemeni journalist **Abdulaziz Muhammad al-Sabri** details the dangers of reporting in his country. Interview by **Laura Silvia Battaglia**

ABDULAZIZ MUHAMMAD AL-SABRI is smiling, despite everything. But he cannot fail to feel depressed when he sees the photos taken a few months ago, in which he is holding a telephoto lens or setting up a video camera on a tripod: "The Houthis confiscated these from me. They confiscated all my equipment. Even if I wanted to continue working, I wouldn't be able to."

Al-Sabri is a Yemeni journalist, filmmaker and cameraman, and a native of Taiz, the city that was briefly the bloodiest frontline in the country's civil war. He has worked in the worst hotspots, supplying original material to international media like Reuters and Sky News. "I have always liked working in the field," he said, "and I was really doing good work from the start of the 2011 revolution."

But since the beginning of the war, the working environment for Yemeni journalists has progressively deteriorated. In the most recent case, veteran journalist Yahia Abdulraqeeb al-Jubaihi faced a trial behind closed doors and was sentenced to death after he published stories critical of Yemen's Houthi rebels. Many journalists have disappeared or been detained, and media outlets closed, in the past few years.

"The media industry and those who work in Yemen are coming up against a war machine which slams every door in our faces, and which controls all the local and international media bureaus. Attacks and assaults against us have affected 80% of the people employed in these professions, without counting the journalists who have already been killed, and there have been around 160 cases of assaults, attacks and kidnappings. Many journalists have had to leave the country to save their lives. Like my very dear friend Hamdan al-Bukari, who was working for Al-Jazeera in Taiz."

Al-Sabri wanted to tell his story to Index on Censorship without leaving out details "because there is nothing left for us to do here except to denounce what is going on, even if nobody is listening to us". He spoke of systematic intimidation by the Houthi militias in his area against journalists in general, and in particular against those who work for the international media: "In Taiz they have even used us as human shields. Many colleagues have been taken to arms depots, which are under attack from the [Saudi-led, government-allied] coalition, so that once the military target has been hit, the coalition can be accused of killing journalists."

This sort of intimidation is one of the reasons why researching and reporting on the conflict is very difficult. "In Taiz and in the north, apart from those working for al-Masirah, the Houthis' TV station, and the pro-Iranian channels, al-Manar and al-Alam, only a few other journalists are able to work from here, and those few, local and international, are putting their necks on the line," said al-Sabri.

In Taiz they have even used us as human shields

"You're lucky if you can make it, otherwise you fall victim to a bullet from the militias, attacks, kidnappings. Foreigners are unable even to obtain visas because of the limitations imposed by [Abdrabbuh Mansour] Hadi's government and the coalition. The official excuse is that the government 'fears' for their lives, since if they were kidnapped, imprisoned or died in a coalition bombardment, it would be the Yemeni government's responsibility."

Al-Sabri has personal experience of the violence against journalists in Yemen. In December 2015, he was wounded in the shoulder by a sniper who was aiming at his head. On another occasion, he was kidnapped, held at a secret location for 15 days, blindfolded, threatened with death and tortured.

"I was abducted a second time, together with my colleague Hamdan al-Bukari, an Al Jazeera reporter, and our driver, on →

OPPOSITE: Journalists stand in front of buildings in Taiz, Yemen, which were destroyed during battles between Houthi fighters and pro-government fighters in November 2016

ABOVE: Photo of Abdulaziz Muhammad al-Sabri taken after he was shot by a sniper

→ 18 January 2016. We had only just left a friend's house to go back to where we lived, when we were blocked in by a car. A group of masked, armed men forced us to leave, hooded us and took us to an unknown location, probably somewhere near the front line, because we could distinctly hear the sound of artillery shells. At three in the morning the following day, the kidnappers separated us. We were still hooded. As far as

At the end of the interrogation, they returned me to the room and said that they would execute me

I was concerned, they did not allow me to remove the blindfold and had I done so, they said that they would have killed me. They brought me some food and I ate it with my eyes closed. I asked who they were and what they wanted and they replied that they were Houthi militiamen, and that I would learn at the right time what was being asked of me.

"The next day they took me to another room for interrogation, and so it went on, every day for 15 days. Whoever interrogated me accused me of betrayal, of working for foreigners, accused me of being a mercenary, someone who took money from the Saudis, Emiratis, Americans and the Muslim Brotherhood, singling me and those like me out as Yemen's public enemy number one. At the end of the interrogation, they returned me to the room and said that they would execute me.

"And they continued like this: they went out and came back in again and said that they would kill me. Every day. I lived through hell, thinking every moment about dying."

To this day al-Sabri still bears the scars of those horrendous 15 days: "After my release, my psychological state was so devastated that I stopped working and practising journalism. Even if I wanted to try again, how could I work if they have destroyed my equipment?"

Al-Sabri does not have much faith in the international community to make things change. "We journalists in Yemen are caught between two systems of ferocious military propaganda: the government's and that of the Houthi rebels. Both factions persecute the journalists who work for the opposite side, besides not recognising the idea of independent journalism. There is no protection whatsoever, either for journalists or for journalism, here. Other than the usual UN representatives who 'express concerns', there is no real intervention from abroad at all.

"I believe that the international community should oblige both factions to give journalists the freedom to speak. They should fight for the full activation in Yemen of Article 19 of the Yemeni Law [from 1990], which guarantees freedom of expression and is against censorship of the press. Otherwise, the situation will remain the same and you will hear of us again, but as people who have died." ⊗

Translated by **Sue Copeland**

Award-winning journalist **Laura Silvia Battaglia** *reports regularly from Yemen*

Novel lines

Jemimah Steinfeld talks to award-winning author **Margaret Atwood** about fake news, silencing scientists and handmaids in Texas

MARGARET ATWOOD HAS a wish. She would like to see a list of martyrs who have been killed for free speech and for those martyrs to somehow be commemorated, either through a statue or a wall.

"These people give their all and then somebody kills them and then we all forget about them," Atwood told Index over the phone from her office in Toronto.

Who would be on Atwood's list? Potentially William Tyndale, a writer and translator of the Bible, who was executed in the 15th century. "Go back a bit; go back in history. You could go back to Socrates." she said.

It's hardly a surprise that Atwood would want some form of commemoration for persecuted writers; the Booker winner is an ardent supporter of free speech. Atwood, who is a long-standing patron of Index on Censorship, received the English PEN Pinter prize in recognition of her work defending writers' rights in 2016. As part of winning the award, she nominated Ahmedur Rashid Chowdhury for the international component, a Bangladeshi publisher who survived a machete and gun attack by Islamic extremists.

Atwood has always been concerned about writers, but right now she is particularly worried about journalists. "I think the most important issues swirl around journalism," she said.

"Take fake news, that's very much an →

ABOVE: Canadian author Margaret Atwood

ABOVE: A scene from the recent TV adaptation of Atwood's The Handmaid's Tale, currently airing in the UK on Channel 4

issue. Mainstream media, however much you deride them, they're at least accountable."

Talking about journalists broadly segues into talking about science journalists specifically. The environment is a recurrent theme in Atwood's work. Pollution contributes to the fertility decline that is the undoing of Gilead in The Handmaid's Tale, while her MaddAddam trilogy imagines a world where the planet's resources are severely depleted.

Atwood is keen to discuss the destruction of the planet past and present. What is perhaps as worrying as the earth's escalating degradation is the recent trend to dismiss research carried out by scientists, particularly environmental scientists, she argued. Atwood mentions Trump's attempts to dismantle the US Environmental Protection Agency.

"We went through that with the [Stephen] Harper government here in this country for about eight or 10 years. He was shutting down and destroying records... He was not interested in having that information out there," she said.

"Even though we were paying for them with public money, they weren't allowed to talk with us. It's pretty frightening."

Frightening indeed as part of the solution lies in the ready flow of information.

"That's why it's important not to shut down science communication because that's where a lot of the solutions are going to come from. Censoring D H Lawrence is one thing, and we couldn't get Lady Chatterley's Lover in Canada until I was an undergrad, but censoring science communication is really important not to do."

Born in Ottawa, Canada, in 1939, Atwood's father, Carl Atwood, was an entomologist, and she spent a lot of her childhood in Canada's wilderness, stationed near insect research centres. She taught herself how to read so that she could consume "the funny papers" as she called them, comics that came with colour supplements in the newspapers in the 1940s and 1950s. "Nobody would read the funny papers to me," she explained.

An avid reader, Atwood started to write and around the age of seven produced her first novel. "It was about an ant. Not an advisable narrative as ants don't do much until the last quarter of their life," she said.

At high school she committed herself to writing more seriously and published her first book of poetry while at the University of Toronto in 1961. Today Atwood's collection of works could probably fill a small library and she is no stranger to different forms and genres. It is the issues, though, of human rights and the environment that have cemented her reputation. At 77 does she believe people get more intolerant with age?

"If you're inclined that way. Some of your tendencies might become more pronounced and you might lose some inhibitions about saying things. I think that people who have been generous when they are 30 are going to be generous when they are 70."

Atwood describes the current climate as "very worrisome". Yet she is remarkably upbeat. In the past she has gone on the record saying all writers are optimists (you've got to be to think your book will sell, she said) and when we speak a sense of positivity shines through. She has a dry chuckle, which is peppered throughout the interview, and for every negative point she has a counter, good one. Take youth, for example. She's concerned about universities, the rise of safe spaces and other trends that might be hindering free speech on campus. She also believes students have lost the art of debate.

"I think it's less well understood. People have kind of forgotten what a debate is; an argued, respectful, well-presented point-of-view instead of name calling," she said. For Atwood social media shoulders a large chunk of the blame for this. "There's a lot of shouting… It fosters knee-jerk reactions without consequences."

But of youth more broadly Atwood feels encouraged. "We were getting a line that young people were apathetic and weren't into politics, and that turns out not to be true. I think the point when they weren't into politics was when it was same old, same old and they didn't see any chance of making a difference and the same old, same old wasn't doing anything that directly riled them up. But quite a few young people seem to be, as they say, 'woken' at the moment."

Fear is part of this waking up moment, as is a ramped-up effort "to stem the flow, as it were". For Atwood, a heartening recent initiative is the appearance of handmaids – female protesters wearing the iconic white bonnets and long, red cloaks – who turned up at the Texas Senate to protest several abortion-related bills.

"That's a spontaneous movement. It's not television organising it, and it's not me organising it." Atwood calls this movement "pretty clever". "Nobody can accuse them of causing a disturbance and they're very modestly dressed and they're silent and everybody knows as soon as they see them exactly what they mean."

That the youth have "woken up" is very reassuring. With a president in the White House who has framed a bullseye around women's reproductive rights and the free press, the world of Gilead is suddenly feeling all too close. And yet, as Atwood explains, the writing was already on the wall when the book was published in 1985.

"I put nothing into it that people had not done at some point or that people weren't already doing. People in the United States at that time on the religious right were already talking about what they would like to do if they had the chance. And that's the reason why it's so relevant today. People have the chance and they're doing those things," Atwood explained.

Hindsight is, of course, a wonderful thing. When The Handmaid's Tale was published, few were concerned that this future dystopia could become reality, at least not in the USA. In 1990 the novel was turned into a film and Atwood went to Berlin for showings. East Berliners watched it intently and commented on its relevance to their life behind the wall.

"They didn't mean the theology or the outfits; they meant not knowing who you could trust," said Atwood. West Berliners, on the other hand, didn't take the plot seriously. For them, said Atwood, "America was still seen as the great and good and home of

Even though we were paying for them with public money, they weren't allowed to talk with us. It's pretty frightening

liberal democracy and they didn't think they would do such a thing".

That assumption not only involved a misunderstanding of the USA, it involved a misunderstanding of humanity and of history.

"As William Gibson says the future is already here – it's just not evenly distributed," Atwood remarked, before adding:

"And so is democracy".

Jemimah Steinfeld is deputy editor at Index

No country for free speech?

Free speech in Germany is being threatened by a toxic mix of rising tensions related to immigration and the influx of refugees, and actions to stop people being upset or offended, writes **Daniel Leisegang**

DEBATES ABOUT HATE speech and fake news are increasingly high profile in Germany. With an election in September, there are rising concerns about the government's response to these, and other trends. Some believe Germany is facing a newly restrictive era for free expression.

The latest threat to free speech is a draft bill passed by the German cabinet in April that threatens social media companies with multi-million euro fines for failing to block content. The government aims to pass the so-called Netzwerkdurchsetzungsgesetz (Network Enforcement Law, abbreviated to NetzDG) by the end of June.

The bill obliges operators of social networks to establish a reporting system for their users. When "obviously illicit" content is reported, the social network has to delete it within 24 hours. If reported content is "not unambiguously illicit" the operators will be given seven days to delete it.

ABOVE: German comedian and talk-show host Jan Böhmermann, who was taken to court for insulting Turkish President Erdogan on his TV show, appears on Late Night with Seth Myers in the USA

If the manager in charge repeatedly fails to block content, they can face fines of up to five million euros ($7,750,295), or up to 50 million euros ($55,359,250) for companies. The definition of what constitutes content that should be removed is vague.

The legislation is meant to tackle illegal hate speech, but is wide enough to include harassment and revilement of religious faith and organisations.

Many free speech advocates oppose the bill because it cuts out courts and other independent bodies from the role of determining legal speech. Matthias Spielkamp, board member of the German section of Reporters Without Borders, said: "Facebook and other social networks are not supposed to become guardians of freedom of expression. It is shameful that the German minister of justice of all people proposes this legislation."

Other critics fear that the draconian penalties will force social media managers to delete content to avoid costs and lengthy trials without any painstaking investigation. The draft bill "will have immense consequences on freedom of speech, especially on completely legal, but unpopular expressions of opinion that will be deleted swiftly," said Ulf Buermeyer, chairman of the Society for Civil Rights. He fears that "the draft bill will pave the way to 'overblocking' in social networks".

Another part of the picture is a softly softly attitude to comedy. Germany's ability to censor satire was put in sharp relief when, in February, a civil court in Hamburg upheld a ruling barring German comedian Jan Böehmermann from repeating parts of a poem, which was rude about Turkey's President Recep Tayyip Erdogan. Boehmermann first caught the media's attention last year when the Turkish embassy called for him to be prosecuted under a little-known law making it illegal to insult foreign leaders.

This move was seen as a way of the Turkish government exporting some of its attitudes to free speech to another country.

However, more encouragingly in January the German government agreed to drop the law that gives special protection to foreign leaders against insults.

Part of the background to this new period of censorship are fears about the global refugee crisis and its political consequences, especially the success of Germany's anti-immigrant party AfD (Alternative für Deutschland).

Since the start of the global displacement crisis in 2015, racism and xenophobia, as well as anti-Islamic and anti-European populism, have grown dramatically in Germany.

The other threat to Germany comes from Russia. Germany's domestic intelligence agency president Hans-Georg Maassen recently warned he has concerns about voters being manipulated by fake news and cited the example of a Russian website carrying

Facebook and other social networks are not supposed to become guardians of freedom of expression

the wholly false story about the father of Martin Schulz, the Social Democrats' candidate for chancellor, having run a Nazi concentration camp.

Maassen has also said there could be a negative influence on the election from the "large amounts of data" supposedly seized by Russian hacker group APT28 during an attack on the country's parliament in 2015.

Fearing further radicalisation on the right, as well as fake news, in September 2015 German minister of justice Heiko Maas set up a task force to combat defamation and deliberate misinformation on social media platforms. Later Maas put more pressure on social networks: "In order to force them to delete illicit content, we need legal obligations." The legislation he proposes to pass in order to do this is NetzDG bill.

HOAXES AND HISTORY

German freedoms of the past 70 years reviewed by SALLY GIMSON

Freedom of speech in Germany is guaranteed under article five of the Grundgesetz (basic law), which forms the basis of the constitution.

Basic law was established in 1949 in the Federal Republic of Germany, four years after the end of World War II. It was part of the groundwork for the formation of a new democratic state and became the constitution for the whole of Germany after reunification in 1990.

According to article five: "Every person shall have the right freely to express and disseminate his opinions in speech, writing and pictures, and to inform himself from generally accessible sources. Freedom of the press and freedom of reporting by means of broadcasts and films shall be guaranteed. There shall be no censorship." The second paragraph, however, goes on to say that free speech may be limited by provisions in other more general laws, and in order to protect young people.

It was not until more than 20 years after the war that the debate about the Nazi period, and who was responsible for the Holocaust and murder of six million Jews and others, really started in German homes. Then, in 1979, the US mini television series Holocaust, about a family in Nazi Germany, was aired on German TV and brought the past into people's living rooms.

In total contrast, a whole pseudo-academic body of literature began to appear on the far right including in 1973, Thies Christophersen's Die Auschwitz-Lüge (The Auschwitz lie); Wilhelm Stäglich's Auschwitz-Mythos (Auschwitz myth) along with non-German works like Arthur Butz's The Hoax of the Twentieth Century. These books claimed the Holocaust and gassing of Jews did not happen.

It was against this background that the German government made Holocaust denial a crime as part of legislation on *Volksverhetzung* (or incitement of hatred). This was challenged in 1994, but was upheld and tightened, and the principle has been subsequently confirmed that "approval, denial, downplaying or justification" of Nazi crimes and the Holocaust, is and remains a criminal offence with a maximum sentence of five years in prison.

→ But in a refreshing sign that people are still fighting for free speech, after the cabinet proposed the NetzDG bill, activists and bloggers published a declaration on freedom of expression. It criticised the government's plans to transfer "predominantly state tasks of enforcement to private companies" and instead called "for a cross-societal approach, which intensifies criminal prosecution and law enforcement while also strengthening counter speech, fostering media literacy, and preserving a regulatory framework that respects freedom of expression in the deletion or blocking of unlawful content".

In May, at the Re:Publica conference on digital society in Berlin, Markus Beckedahl, co-founder of Re:Publica called upon people to "show civil courage on the internet and to fight for an open society that prioritises basic rights, democracy and state of law".

Nothing less should be on the agenda of the German government. Whether the NetzDG contributes to this goal is doubtful. ⊗

Daniel Leisegang is a political scientist and editor of Blätter für deutsche und internationale Politik

Read all about it

Somaliland's rapidly expanding book fair is soon to open as the region copes with one of its worst droughts, reports **Julia Farrington**

SOMALILAND'S HARGEYSA INTERNATIONAL book fair is marking its 10th anniversary this July, with the largest cultural event the city will have seen for more than 40 years. But although the rains have now started, the fair is taking place against the backdrop of a catastrophic drought.

Jama Musse Jama, director of Redsea Cultural Foundation and founder of the fair, said that normally they would have launched the fair by now but "all of our volunteers have all gone to the most extremely affected areas of the drought. They are helping where they can, putting up shelters, helping to distribute food and the situation is made worse by disease".

ABOVE: Women browse books at the Hargeysa Book Fair in 2015, which has grown from a few hundred attendees to thousands in a matter of years

ABOVE: A view of Hargeysa, Somaliland

But he and the other organisers hope the situation will improve rapidly, as the first rains have now begun to fall. "The book fair is scheduled and we do not see possibilities to cancel," Jama assured Index as we went to press.

The drought has been a disaster for Somaliland, a self-declared state that is an autonomous region of Somalia but now has its own parliament and institutions. It considers

Every region of Somaliland now has, or plans to have, a library

itself the successor to the British Somaliland protectorate. According to a UN report in March, across Somaliland and wider Somalia more than 2.9 million people were facing crisis conditions and needing emergency food aid in the worst drought to hit the region in decades.

The book fair, however, represents cultural and artistic pride in Somaliland and is aimed at inspiring its large young population. Its significance can be best understood against the backdrop of the state's ongoing struggle for independence and international recognition as a nation state.

The fair is a success by any standards. It has grown from 200 attendees in 2008 to 11,000 in 2016, despite the ongoing war in the region that threatens its stability and the chilling effect of a fatwa issued against the organisers in 2015.

Jama believes in Somaliland, where there is such a focus on development, humanitarian issues and often pressing needs for basic life necessities such as food, health services and shelter, the risk is forgetting that art and culture is fundamental to society.

He recently wrote: "This risk, in particular, affects disproportionately young people who have little employment opportunities and hence economic means to meet their basic needs, but also lack access to alternative engaging avenues. Take as an example Hargeysa, where almost all of its one million population, mostly young, has no access to art (theatre, libraries, museums etc). In such circumstances it is inevitable that unemployed and disenfranchised youth can be susceptible to radicalisation, criminality

CREDIT: HomoCosmicos/iStock

and migration as a way out of escaping from hardships of life."

For the first time the literary festival will take place across the whole city, instead of at just one venue. "It will be a collective celebration of the city and of the people," Jama explained. "We will run parallel sessions in the university, major hotels, cafes, outside the city, by the sea and sessions for children. We have the new Hargeysa Cultural Centre, which is another reason to celebrate, and hopefully the National Theatre of Hargeysa is ready."

The fair's popularity is driven by a vision to inspire new writers and readers of all ages in one of the world's newest written languages. Somali became a written language in 1973 when the euphoria of the post-colonial period fuelled a cultural renaissance.

But with the catastrophic events of the intervening years, including the destruction of the capital Hargeysa in 1991 and subsequent ensuing conflict, the majority of the country had no access to books until the fair started in 2008. As part of the fair's wider mission, Redsea created a year-round mobile library programme. The library travels across the country, including to the most remote communities, supporting reading and writing groups. Groups of young people from reading clubs around the country are bussed in to the capital each year to the festival to take part in workshops, panels and lectures.

Every region of Somaliland now has, or plans to have, a library. As Ayan Mayamoud, co-director of the fair, explained: "Cultural spaces make it possible for young people to come together to develop shared values and to grow as responsible citizens. They contribute to development and economic growth but also to peace and stability."

Acting as a magnet and a conduit for writers, artists, performers, translators, publishers and, of course, books from all over Africa and around the world, the book fair has also triggered huge change in Hargeysa.

Hamdi Ali came to the first fair when still in high school. She is now librarian of the Hargeysa Cultural Centre. She said: "Now there are five amazing bookshops in Hargeysa, stocking titles in Somali and English, where before only religious books were available in Arabic. Lots of books are published locally and there are two main publishing houses." It is clear that the fair has transformed her life too: "Like you might see a diamond but you might not be interested in it unless someone tells you – this is a diamond and it is really expensive. Books were like that for me and the book fair showed me their value."

And she's not the only one. Hamdi claimed the fair has given birth to at least 15 published writers.

Jama said: "The book was always an excuse because we celebrate all forms of

There are five amazing bookshops in Hargeysa, stocking titles in Somali and English, where before only religious books were available

arts – music, painting, poetry, of course. Somalilanders believe that they are all poets. Having all these things around the book community is what makes it unique, and connects very strongly with the younger generation."

With so much to celebrate on the one hand and the scale of the humanitarian disaster on the other, the organisers face a dilemma. Mayamoud, like all the organisers, is deeply affected by the drought, but insists that life must go on. "Art and culture are a fundamental part of human life. If you leave out culture, you leave out a vital part of what it is to be human, and we need poets and artists to bring us together at this time."

Julia Farrington is an associate arts producer at Index on Censorship

See no evil

A backlash against reporters covering Chechnya's persecution of gay men highlights the dangers of getting truth out in this corrupt state. A Chechen journalist speaks out about the challenges

ONLY ONE RULE governs journalists' work in Chechnya: we are all part of Ramzan Kadyrov's press service. After Kadyrov came to power in 2007 as the country's head of the republic, the media was turned into his personal propaganda tool. I almost lost my job once for using footage in a news story showing former president of the republic Alu Alkhanov, Kadyrov's predecessor. Alkhanov is politically sound, but Kadyrov doesn't like him. Because of this, Alkhanov's name cannot be mentioned. In another instance, I recorded an interview with a man who was tortured by the Chechen authorities. After the interview came out, the man had to flee the country to ensure his safety. I still think it's my fault.

Journalists here now know what they can and cannot write in order to stay safe and survive. Sadly, what they can write doesn't amount to much. The main news topic for any publication is Kadyrov, his family and his relatives. There is virtually no story emanating from the Chechen media that fails to mention the name Kadyrov. It might refer to the head of Chechnya himself; his father, who was assassinated in 2004; his mother, who heads a charitable foundation; or his wife and children. This is the case for stories on politics right the way through to sport. For example, a headline might run saying Kadyrov attended the rehearsal of a dance ensemble, praised the artists or handed the soloist the keys to a car or even an apartment. Another might say Kadyrov attended the annual mixed martial arts tournament in Grozny or show Kadyrov visiting a hospital and distributing envelopes containing money to patients. The only time when the head of Chechnya is not mentioned in the news is during the weather report.

Television is used not only as propaganda but as a tool of intimidation. The stories that appear to get the most attention show people apologising to Kadyrov for having complained about the authorities. This is how it goes: on social media, someone complains about the authorities, talking about corruption, salaries being withheld or a kidnapping. The complaint is seen by the authorities, who find and beat up or threaten the author, turn on a camera and force an apology.

Here's another example. When Kadyrov started using Instagram, Chechens saw his presence on the social network as an opportunity to address him directly. Seeing that he gave apartments, cars and expensive gifts to distinguished people, citizens told him about real problems, such as being homeless, having a sick child or being unemployed or severely underpaid. Kadyrov responded to almost every message. A special group contacted the author of each request, went to the relevant address and found out what the situation was. At first glance, everything looked humane, but in fact this group was

The only time when the head of Chechnya is not mentioned in the news is during the weather report

created in order to protect Kadyrov from the authors' problems. Often "verification" ended with a report, aired on TV, claiming the person was an idler or an imposter.

There is also a troll farm in Chechnya. The organisation is located in one of the buildings of the Grozny-City complex. It employs a dozen people who monitor the Chechen and Russian media constantly and write comments on anything concerning Kadyrov or Chechnya. If the news is positive, the organisation's employees confirm it. If the news is bad, they refute it. In one instance, a "comment" written by someone who went by the name of Nikolai from Arkhangelsk read: "I came back from Chechnya yesterday. There are no kidnappings. People all love Kadyrov. Grozny is the safest city in the world."

For the work of trolling, employees →

OPPOSITE: Chechenya's head of the republic Ramzan Kadyrov speaks to the media after a suicide bombing in 2014

are paid handsomely. Some media employees also receive bonuses if they post good news about Chechnya on social media.

There are independent media outlets from Russia and elsewhere who operate in Chechnya, but their work is difficult, too. Kadyrov repeatedly says that media outlets such as Russian Ekho Moskvy, Novaya Gazeta, RBC, Dozhd and Latvia-based Meduza are treacherous, hostile and pursuing the collapse of the country. For example, when, in March, Novaya Gazeta published a series of investigative articles reporting that men suspected of being homosexual were being rounded up and tortured in secret prisons, the news was quickly denied. Alvi Karimov, Kadyrov's spokesman, called Novaya Gazeta's report "an absolute lie" in an interview with Russia's state-funded Interfax

Ordinary people are too afraid to talk to journalists and officials simply refuse to do so

news agency, saying there were no gay men in Chechnya to be persecuted.

It's not just being discredited that is a threat. There are real dangers to reporters. Journalists from these publications are almost always watched and intimidated, and are sometimes killed. Two journalists at Novaya Gazeta have been murdered while covering stories from Chechnya over the past two decades, and the reporter who covered the homosexuality stories has been threatened. At a gathering on 3 April of about 15,000 men, Kadyrov's adviser Adam Shahidov called the Novaya Gazeta journalists "enemies of our faith and our motherland" and promised "vengeance", according to the CPJ.

Then there are the difficulties of finding people to interview. Ordinary people are too afraid to talk to journalists and officials simply refuse to do so. These news outlets cannot have anonymous stringers in Chechnya because it is almost impossible to maintain anonymity. Chechnya is small; everybody knows everybody. Journalists can hide their own name, but in order to do normal journalistic work they need to interview people, to provide details, to describe an event that took place. Through details it is very easy to understand about what and about whom an article was written. Knowing what the Chechen authorities are capable of when quashing dissent, no one wants to put at risk someone who merely agrees to be interviewed.

Even the foreign press is suffering. Until recently, it was well represented and foreign journalists often came and conducted interviews. People spoke more easily with them, perhaps because the articles were published in foreign languages and were rarely translated. But the situation changed dramatically in March 2016 when a group of journalists travelling with human rights activists were beaten up and severely injured in the neighbouring republic of Ingushetia. Their vehicle was burned and they ended up in hospital. No one had any doubt the attackers had acted on the order of the Chechen authorities. After this incident, few foreign journalists have risked going to Chechnya. Without them, there's even less hope for reporting what is going on honestly in Chechnya. ⊗

The writer of this article is from Chechnya and has worked in the media there for more than a decade. They wish to remain anonymous for security reasons

No laughing matter

Spanish authorities are increasingly cracking down on public criticism, with comedians amongst those most at risk, writes **Silvia Nortes**

SPANISH COMEDIAN DANI Mateo referred to the Valle de los Caídos (Valley of the Fallen), a monument built by Franco's regime, as "shit" last May. He did it during a satirical television show, but the Asociación para la Defensa del Valle de los Caídos (the Association for the Defence of the Valley of the Fallen) accused him of insulting religious feelings. A year later, this May, Mateo has been called to testify before a judge.

"This is stupid and no decent tribunal would condemn him," said Spanish comedian Miguel Lago. "I would tell the judiciary to prosecute criminals, not comedians."

This is the latest in a series of recent prosecutions against journalists, comedians and social network users that have raised the alarm on the health of freedom of expression in Spain. The legal framework that is allowing these prosecutions has been pushed through by the party currently in power, Partido Popular.

These developments might find their roots in popular unrest. An increase in corruption cases, money laundering and influence peddling among members of the Partido Popular – in power since 2011 – has led to protests and growing criticism of the government →

ABOVE: A man at a protest against the government's new security law in Madrid in February, 2015

on social media and by journalists and comedians. With new political movements such as Podemos or Ciudadanos also adding to the pressure on the establishment, this political flux could be motivating behind the increase in prosecutions.

Virginia Álvarez, homeland policy spokeswoman for Amnesty International, said the citizen security law, passed in 2015, caused a public outcry because it "allows the prosecution of journalists for reporting police interventions… which attacks the right to inform". The law was passed in parliament with the votes of the conservative Partido Popular, but with no support from other parties.

Moreover, the 2015 reforms created a range of terrorism offences. For example, "glorifying terrorism", under article 578, allows a wide interpretation and is left to the mercy of judges. Last year, two puppeteers were jailed over a satirical performance in Madrid that included a sign with the word "alka-ETA", a combination of al-Qaeda and Basque separatist group ETA. Article 510, which punishes hate crimes, is also being used to limit citizens' rights.

The reforms were made to fight jihadist terrorism which, as stated in the penal code, "includes new forms of aggression by using new recruitment and indoctrination instruments". Álvarez denounced this reasoning. "This is not preventing terrorism crimes but allowing the state to act against humorous comments," she said. "Governments are using the insecurity caused by terrorism to curb freedoms and deactivate social movements."

Thousands of people have protested against the changes, and human rights groups and the Spanish opposition have fiercely opposed it. There has also been a ratcheting up of criticism in the media, with a growing number of critical editorials and commentary. This, in turn, has led to more prosecutions, creating a vicious circle.

Facu Díaz, a comedian who was prosecuted last year for posting jokes on Twitter, said: "The same court is judging jihadists and people that post jokes." For Díaz, police involvement in itself is a matter of concern. "They don't have experience in social media. It's like giving a gun to a monkey."

These legal proceedings seem to be aimed at challenging media support for the accused. "There is great pressure, and judges feel they have to set an example, even though it might be unpopular. Otherwise, [this] might not have led to prison sentences," said Raúl Pardo, a leading criminal lawyer.

Comedian and actor Álex O'Dogherty said: "These attacks are trying to make us afraid of raising our voices. Who decides what constitutes an offence? We need to worry about facts, not words."

Mateo's case is just one of several that worry freedom-of-expression defenders. In April, 21-year-old Cassandra Vera was sentenced to a year in prison for posting jokes about Luis Carrero Blanco, the president during the last years of Franco's dictatorship who was murdered by ETA in 1973. Also in April, three women were accused of a "religious hate crime" for mocking an Easter procession in Seville by carrying a giant plastic vagina as a feminist protest.

This repressive path is threatening social agitators and free thinkers, and therefore the exercising of democratic rights.

Despite all this, there is room for hope. "Spain will never lose its sense of humour," said comedian Ana Morgade. "We are stripping comedy of what makes it funny… But this does not mean we cannot retrace our steps." ⊗

Silvia Nortes is a journalist based in Spain

> **The same court is judging jihadists and people that post jokes**

Cementing dissatisfaction

Protesters casting their feet in concrete are grabbing attention in Indonesia. Now they are inspiring other communities to challenge the government using new tactics, reports **Eliza Vitri Handayani**

IT STARTED OFF as an 11-person protest. Women from central Java, wearing traditional clothes and farmers' hats, sat in front of the presidential palace in Jakarta this March and put their feet in wet concrete until it set. The boxes the women planted their feet in came to just above their ankles.

They couldn't move around and needed to be lifted to go to the toilet. At the end of each day, the women were ferried to the nearby Legal Aid Foundation office in Jakarta, where they would sleep with their feet still embedded in concrete blocks. They would then repeat the protest. The protesters sat in the sun and rain, singing songs, saying prayers. Soon some 60 people had joined them, all encasing their feet in cement. All refused to break the concrete until they could meet with the president. Six days into this unusual protest their wish was granted.

ABOVE: Activists hold a mock burial to commemorate Patmi, who died during the March 2017 protest

CREDIT: Afriadi Hikmal/Barcoft Images/Getty Images

ABOVE:
Villagers from the March 2017 protest

→ The protest is part of a series of demonstrations organised by communities around the Kendeng ridge, which spans 250 kilometres in northern Java. The ridge is abundant in limestone and clay, essential for making cement, and has been eyed up by large corporations. But the area is also home to many farmers who own, cultivate and depend on its fertile lands.

"We want to show the president and the nation that our livelihood and our lives are being threatened by cement companies," said Sukinah, one of the protesters, in an interview with Index.

Following the protests, an environmental study on Kendeng has been ordered by the government. It is due out in June.

The inventiveness of these protests has inspired others. Many communities have recently visited the Kendeng villages to study their methods, including Aleta Baun, who staged her own protest in 2013 in Timor where villagers occupied local marble mining sites and weaved. Baun visited in April to learn more about the Kendeng people and to swap tips on successful activism.

Ibrahim Massindereng, a lawyer for the Association of the Defenders of Traditional Communities, has been involved with the people of Seko, on the island of Sulawesi, since 2015. He told Index that one person from Seko, Andri Karyo, had visited Kendeng and that people from Seko had gathered locally to watch the protests on tapes. Massindereng said: "Women stepped forward; around 400 women set up and manned tents for 2 months at the planned hydroelectric dam site. Before Andri's visit to Kendeng, Seko's women were rarely involved." With a theatrical background, Massindereng is preparing a dramatic protest, "a harvest party," which he said he was coordinating with artists in the area.

And there have already been protests inspired by Kendeng. For example, at the end of March a protest was mounted by Forum Satu Bumi (One Earth Forum) in the city of Samarinda, East Kalimantan, to voice their concerns on how this province in Borneo has been destroyed by the mining of oil, gas and coal. They also put their feet in concrete.

"We meet often, in different villages, sometimes a few times a week," said Giyem talking about how the Kendeng protesters organise. She is a farmer and leader in her Pati village. "There are always representatives from the different villages."

"We usually don't plan far ahead of time," said Sukinah. "We decided to cement our feet a few days before we left for Jakarta."

Dhyta Caturani, a Jakarta activist involved in the Kendeng struggle, confirmed this. "One morning they told us they were going to Jakarta and we scrambled to find them a place to stay," she told Index. To fund campaigns each village has set up a reserve. "Each time we want to do something, everyone contributes," said Sukinah.

Dewi Candraningrum paints portraits of the farmers, to increase their profile. She has painted Kendeng leaders such as Joko Prianto and Paini; those criminalised for protesting, like Murtini; and those who died during the Kendeng people's 10-year struggle so far like Atma Khikmi Azmy, who was killed in an accident; and Sarmi, who was killed by a sickle to the neck by a pro-cement thug.

"It's as if the dead are still fighting beside us, which is in line with Samin belief that when people die they simply take a different form," said Candraningrum.

Many artists have created works and

donated the proceeds to support the Kendeng cause, including well-known band Marjinal, graphic artists, tattoo artists, T-shirt makers and batik artists. The documentary Samin vs Semen was shown in Germany this year by Dandhy Laksono, the director, and Gunarti, a Pati farmer who was instrumental in bringing women into the struggle.

Kendeng farmers have been politically active for 10 years since a traditional Samin community in Pati resisted plans to set up a mining operation in their village. They rallied support and founded a network of allies. Over the years they have pursued legal means, as well as frequently holding events with strong messages and creative methods rooted in local culture and spirituality. The women who encased their feet in concrete had campaigned before. In April 2015, they had beaten *lesung* – a wooden vessel and pestles, used to grind rice – in front of the presidential palace.

"We wished to wake the Indonesian government to our plight and beat back environmental destruction caused by cement companies," said Sukinah.

Significantly, nine of them already had encased their feet in concrete last year. This protest ended after they met the president's staff and were promised a meeting. The meeting never materialised, but they realised it was an effective means of getting their message out. They camped outside the president's palace again later and finally met him.

The meeting and the ensuing study did briefly halt some plans. But when a cement company's licence was reissued this February in Rembang, the women returned to Jakarta.

They were joined by dozens more people from their villages, as well as sympathisers from Jakarta and Papua. The women's persistence in demonstrating had captured much public attention. Expressions of solidarity poured in from Sumatra, Kalimantan, Sulawesi and abroad.

Not everyone supports the protests though. Some accused the Kendeng farmers of abusing women by forcing them to encase their feet in cement. "We put women forward because we want to avoid tendencies towards violence," said Sukinah. "No one was obligated to take on any roles, everyone volunteered," Giyem added. This included Patmi, a protester who died of a heart attack the night after she removed her feet. Her widower Rosat told Index: "The struggle to preserve mother earth was very important to her. She participated in all kinds of protests."

Many accused the women of being bad mothers who abandoned their children. "We're doing this for our children too, so we can keep our lands to bequeath to them," said Sukinah.

Intimidation by thugs and officials, criminalisation of protesters and media bias have all happened. There are demonstrators and

All refused to break the concrete until they could meet with the president

social media campaigners paid by pro-cement interests. Children are bullied at school by pro-cement teachers. There have been sexual assaults on women activists.

"Historically Samin people have resisted exploitation. If anyone says we're violating Samin philosophy, then they haven't understood it completely," said Gunretno, a prominent Kendeng leader, in an interview with Index.

Siti, a Samin farmer, added, "I don't think I'm violating our customs. Our purpose in protesting is clear: to protect the land. Samin people are allowed to work only as farmers. If our lands are lost, if our water runs dry, it hurts us and everyone in the region."

Eliza Vitri Handayani is an author and translator. Her novel From Now On Everything Will Be Different *was published in 2015*

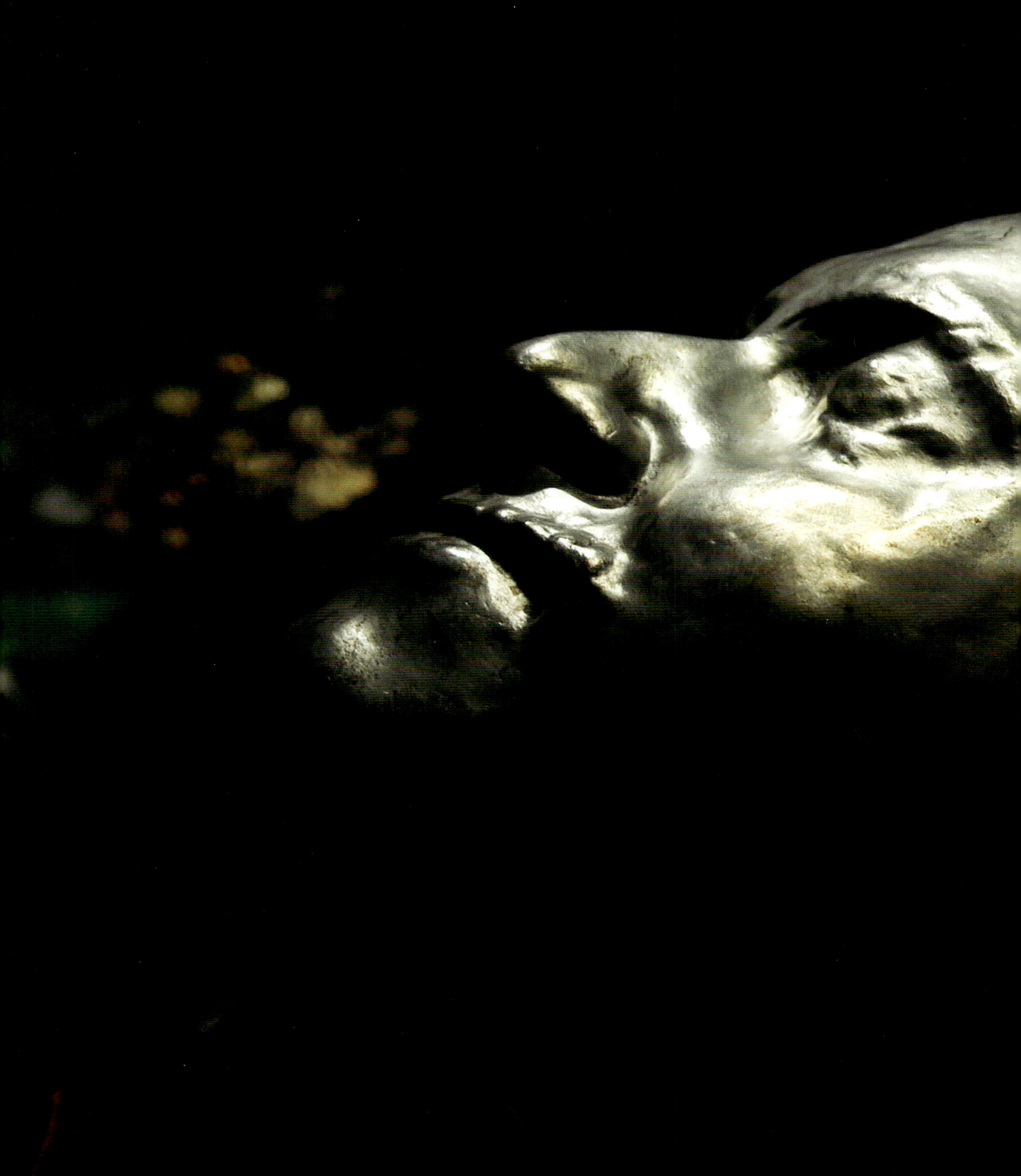

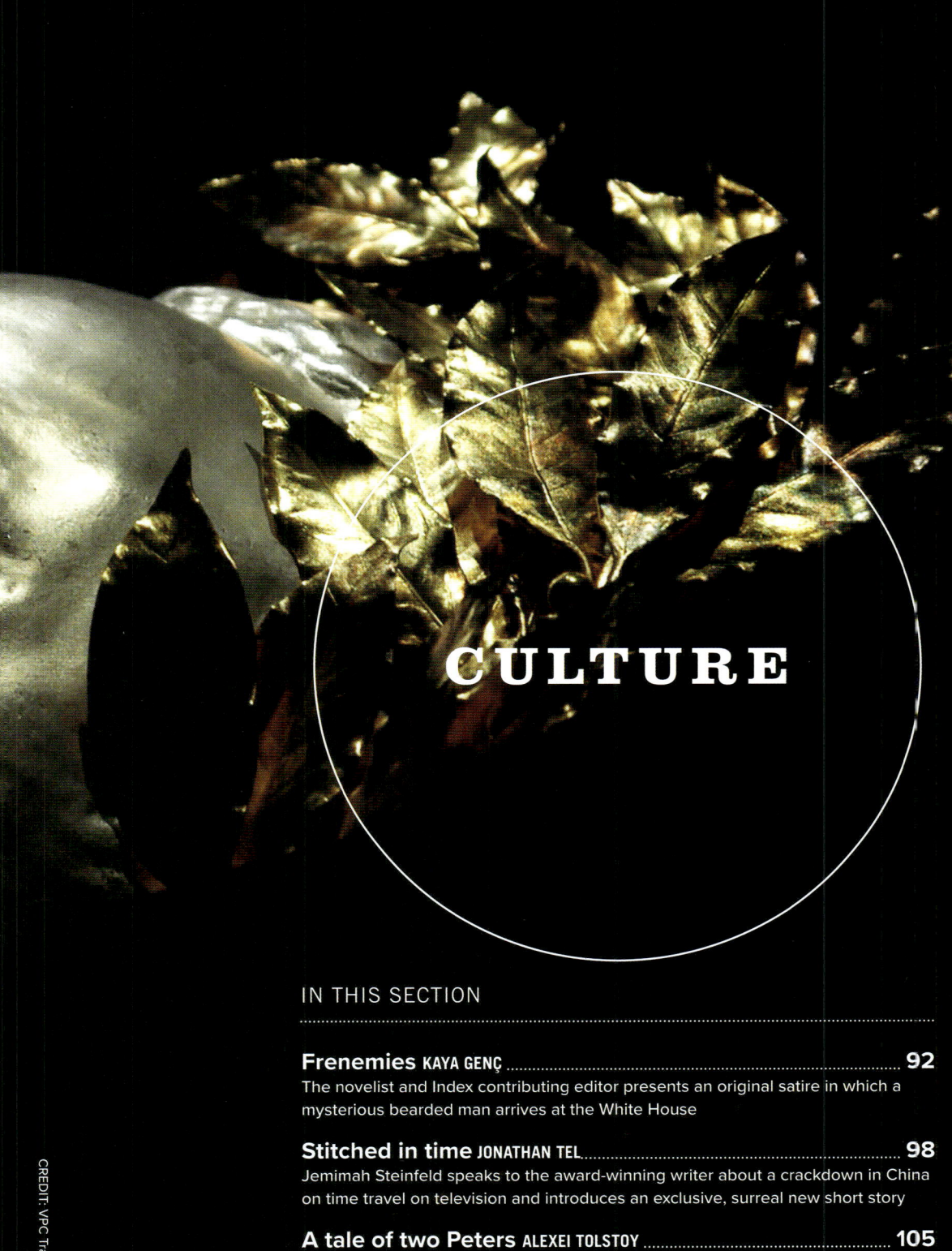

CULTURE

IN THIS SECTION

Frenemies KAYA GENÇ **92**
The novelist and Index contributing editor presents an original satire in which a mysterious bearded man arrives at the White House

Stitched in time JONATHAN TEL **98**
Jemimah Steinfeld speaks to the award-winning writer about a crackdown in China on time travel on television and introduces an exclusive, surreal new short story

A tale of two Peters ALEXEI TOLSTOY **105**
The Comrade Count's novel Peter the Great was liked by Stalin, who saw favourable parallels to his own leadership. Boris Dralyuk introduces Tolstoy's earlier, less flattering portrayal of the tsar, translated into English for the first time

MAIN: Death mask of Tsar Peter the Great seen at the State Historical Museum of Russia, Moscow

Frenemies

A strange man arrives at the White House. What does he want? Index's contributing editor **Kaya Genç** presents a satirical short story, written exclusively for the magazine, which re-imagines a new political alliance

THE BEARDED MAN appeared mysteriously one December evening before the concealed white doors of the Oval Office. It was the butler who first talked to him. The pale-faced man was carrying an old edition of Notes from Underground with him. The butler, meanwhile, had a can of Coke on his tray; the president had acquired a habit of using the red button on his desk for Coke on demand.

"The president had just buzzed me," the butler said irritably, as if talking about a wasp that had just stung him.

Inspecting the stranger's clothes, his irritation grew and he wondered whether he could be an intruder. The middle-aged, silver-bearded stranger looked like he could be one of those radicals whom the French call "*existentialiste*"; he was not only suspiciously silent, but also dressed like an outsider, all in black. His face told the butler that the world was a wicked, wicked place, and no sip of Coke could alter the fact.

Once inside, the butler was surprised to see his orange-skinned boss get to his feet immediately, like a child whose schoolmaster had just entered the classroom. He had never seen the Commander-in-Chief this excited. Even when his wife, who was often away, came to visit, he would refuse to show emotion, sitting in his chair not unlike the recently reinstalled bust of Winston Churchill.

"Here comes the Underground Man!" he exclaimed, as if this could be the actual name of the visitor. "The architect of so many wonderful *things*. You are a brilliant, brilliant person. So good to have you here in the West Wing. So amazingly good to have you in *my room*. The last time I saw you, we were eating hot wings at the Moscow KFC, isn't that right? Brilliant wings, so brilliant they were."

There was a touch of sadness in his voice, the despair of a man for whom the Underground Man and Colonel Sanders could exist on the same plane of significance.

"You are an amazing human being. I remember so detailedly what you said about the Judeo-Christian tradition that day, and something about how important it was, *it is*, for →

CULTURE

us to preserve it. A philosopher – someone who lives with ideas – that is who you are. So tell me, Underground Man, would you like some Coke?"

"Coke is what I came here for, Mr President," the middle-aged man said in a thick Russian accent. His beard had turned grey, but the man's ruffled hair retained its dark colour. "And to give some advice about the *shape of things to come*, too," he added, as if his upcoming policy advice was merely an afterthought to his desire for Coke.

"I hate asking people for things, Coke or otherwise. I want to belong to this age truthfully, without any illusions. Every man for himself, right? That is the mantra of our age. Life designed only for the fittest. The pains of existence pouring on the dispossessed like acid rains. What a compassionless world we live in, and how good to be aware of it. The sad thing is no one is allowed to say it: the world is only for the fittest. But I am getting beyond myself. Can I sit down, Mr President? I have had a long day."

"Tell me about it," his friend replied. "I have been *roasted* from 6am to 11pm today by the fucking CNN, the foolish NBC, the fart-like ABC and the failing Times. They accuse me of being in bed with you, by which I mean *the Russians*. You can never please those furious liberals, can you? They loved Lenin and accused American folks of not understanding the great

What a compassionless world we live in, and how good to be aware of it. The sad thing is no one is allowed to say it: the world is only for the fittest

Russian revolutionaries. Now, those ex-Reds hate Russia and accuse other American folks of collaborating with Russians."

"Call it by its name, Mr President. Call it by its true name. Call it 'condescension'."

"Yes, plain and simple condescension against the kind of people who …" He mumbled a word which the butler couldn't hear. "The kind of people who drink Coke, I guess, despite the baseless accusations by liberals concerning its health implications."

The mysterious man uttered "liberals" with such difficulty that the butler thought the word was hurting his tongue. "Don't forget to always associate condescension with liberals. We are in the midst of a *world-historical* struggle between liberals and the ordinary folk. Never, ever forget that, Mr President. Read Turgenev, Fathers and Sons; read Tolstoy, What Men Live By; read Dostoyevski, Notes from Underground, to better see what I mean. Now, the shallow liberals can't appreciate our Russian depths. They can't see the light in Comrade Stalin's works, either! And it is left to us, Mr President, to carry on with their ideas. You are carrying a massive Russian torch here."

He waited for his friend to imagine the size of what he'd just described. "You and I are freedom-of-expression revolutionaries when you come to think of it," he continued in a passionate voice, as if what he said was an indisputable fact. "Our enemies will no-platform anyone who shares our Judeo-Christian mindset. Write this down: 'They can't stand the messy business of tradition and religion.' This is your ticket for the second term."

"Let me tweet this. I couldn't put it better. You are a true original. You are an amazing individual."

The butler liked what he heard, except for the Stalin bit – that man had built labour camps, had he not? – and felt ashamed for having judged the Underground Man. But then, much to his chagrin, the stranger who claimed to be no different than a Russian peasant brought out a little metal stash from his jacket pocket, split some salt-like stuff on the president's desk, and started dividing it into three lines of equal size with his earth-coloured GUEST ACCESS card. He turned to the President. "You need to do this before hearing out what I have to tell you. You need to relax, sir."

"But that's disgusting," the leader of the free world said. "I have been eating all kinds of things on this table. How can you even consider putting your nostrils on it and breathing in the history of this desk, so to speak?"

"*My President*'s desk is much dirtier," came the reply. "I have even seen pieces of paprika

'They can't stand the messy business of tradition and religion.' This is your ticket for the second term

Pringles there. Just trust me with this, for it is impossible for you to comprehend what I am about to tell you without getting high. You can trust me. You did trust me. You will trust me."

When he woke up the next day, the butler couldn't quite remember what had happened after he was given an executive order to lock the door, sniff a line and lay down on the sofa. The conversation between his boss and the visitor featured hotels, video tapes, golden showers and cameras. In his mind, the butler pictured shiny yellow lines leading up to the sky, all the way to Almighty God, so beautiful was this feeling of transcendence … from that vantage point, everything appeared so small to him, so useless and devoid of significance: Washington DC, the Monument, the White House, his tiny Ford parked outside, the president's hands …

* * *

The leader of the free world was enjoying his well-done steak that March day when the butler entered the concealed rooms of the Oval Office with a can of Coke on his tray at 12.30pm sharp. It was a Monday and the Underground Man, by now a senior advisor to the president, was reading the latest issue of Pravda on the sofa.

→ The Underground Man extended his arm toward the butler to ask for an ashtray. "I have told Kremlin about this *mess* and they agree with my solution." He spat a wad of strawberry-flavoured gum onto the ashtray.

"I call this strategy 'Traces for No Traces', Mr President. The best way to get rid of an old 'trace' is to manufacture a new one. You know about these secret workplace lovers: she is married to her high school sweetheart and he is married with two kids. They get enormous joy from hiding their romance. Once people find out, the banality of the whole thing is revealed to both: he is attractive just because he is forbidden and vice versa. And so, what is the best way to conceal the affair? To appear as enemies, of course. They fight in front of others, raising their voices, accusing each other of doing unmentionable things. This very smoothly removes all doubts concerning their affair, without leaving any trace."

"You are an amazing *individual*," the president said, leaving his half-finished steak on the plate. He had been losing his appetite a lot lately, missing his carefree days. He then ordered the butler to bring him two cans of Coke. "You are an individual," he said, not aware of the word he had forgotten to repeat.

You have to hit your lover straight in the face, you have to rape your love, you have to pull her by the hair and strangle her

* * *

The butler would keep the memory of the stroll that day at the Rose Garden dear for many years to come. It was the first week of April and the 30 different types of tulips crisscrossed around him with boxwood had turned the garden into a festive place. The butler looked at the diamond-shaped lavenders around the crabapple trees and felt lucky to be spending this sunny day in the garden, taking joy at the view of the West Wing colonnade behind them.

For the president, however, all this had little meaning: even that abundance of colour and fragrance were failing to lift his spirits. He seemed like a lost man, walking aimlessly along the pathways, his blue eyes raising to the sky in the pose of a tragic hero looking for an ancient god to rescue him from his sadness.

The Underground Man, who never left his sight in the previous three months, asked the butler to follow them as they moved along the lawn.

"You have your Coke and your policy advice and the support of the world's dispossessed," he told the president in such a sweet, serene tone that he appeared indiscernible from a high school BFF.

"The world's citizens who are brave enough to question climate change, cosmopolitan values and the liberal mindset have put their trust in you, Mr President. I want you to imagine a young French boy who is crying in his room at this very moment. He can't tell his school mates how wrong it is to treat homosexuality as a normal thing: he knows he is right, but he can't voice his opinions, fearing reprisals. Now, I want you to imagine in a lavatory in Berlin this German girl, this tiny beauty, who knows Islam is a hateful religion: it is so obvious to her, but she can't say it aloud ... These people need your urgent support, Mr President. And how can you support them?"

"*How*," the president mumbled with a melancholy voice, as if asked to name a poem.

"Here is *how*. By bombing Syria. By bombing the hell out of them."

"But Syria is not ... Why should I bomb Russia? Syria is Russia. You want me to bomb Russia?"

"This is how desire works, Mr President, this is what Russian literature has taught us for so many decades. You have to hit your lover straight in the face, you have to rape your love, you have to pull her by the hair and strangle her. Only this way she will truly love you ... That is the sad truth of our existence. You should bomb Syria like crazy, Mr President. You should destroy our fighter jets, burn a field or two. Only the sight of that beautiful destruction can lead to a true regeneration."

And with that, the butler saw the leader of the free world smile for the first time after many weeks of frustration and sadness. To the butler's eyes, he seemed wise and strong. In the following hour, he would follow the president as he walked back to the Oval Office and gave the order to bomb, bomb, bomb. He would watch him press a red button, not dissimilar to the one he used for his Coke needs, to forget about the sadness of his existence. He would witness him saving all those innocent children, innocent babies — babies, little babies — from dying.

Kaya Genç *is a novelist and essayist from Istanbul. He is the author of* Under the Shadow, *published in the UK in 2016*

Stitched in time

Award-winning short story writer **Jonathan Tel** often reflects on China's history. Here, he speaks to **Jemimah Steinfeld** about why the government wanted to ban time travel in fiction and introduces a story he has written exclusively for the magazine

THE CHINESE CARE deeply about their past, but the Chinese government wants to control what narrative the public hear, said Jonathan Tel when Index on Censorship spoke to him about his new short story. The story describes a scenario where an actor in a time travel show gets stuck in 19th century Beijing after the government's decision to axe the genre. It's a fictional take on true life. In 2011 the Chinese government did ban all time travel-themed TV.

These TV shows, which typically featured someone from the present going back to the Qing dynasty (1644-1912) or Chinese republic (1912-49), were very popular. Different production companies churned out episodes often. Therein lay the problem; they became very hard for the government to control.

"Time travel TV was chaotic. The Chinese Communist Party only want their narrative of the past," said Tel. This narrative is singular; China is a country full of corrupt feudal overlords and emperors until the nation is saved in 1949 by the CCP.

When the ban came into play, the State Administration of Radio, Film and Television announced it was because the genre "disrespects history". It said: "Producers and writers are treating serious history in a frivolous way, which should by no means be encouraged anymore."

The time travel ban coincided with the 90th anniversary of the founding of the CCP. Another piece of guidance from SARFT was: "Follow the central spirit of the CPC [Communist Party of China] to celebrate its 90th anniversary on television. All levels should actively prepare to launch vivid reproductions of the Chinese revolution, the nation's construction and its reform and opening up."

For Tel the fuss about China's past makes sense. "Chinese history is very relevant to today. People often make comparisons between current situations with those of the past. And so it was not totally crazy for the Chinese government to be concerned about these time travel shows," he said.

Tel won the Commonwealth short story prize in 2015 and the Sunday Times short story prize in 2016 for The Human Phonograph, a tale about a couple living in a remote nuclear base in 1960s China. His research came from memoirs and works by historians, and then his imagination filled any gaps. The Human Phonograph is part of a wider collection about China and is the result of Tel living in the country on and off

ABOVE: Award-winning short story writer Jonathan Tel

for decades. He told Index how censorship has become worse recently. "The things you can read today are less than before. I was reading blogs from Xinjiang and they've sort of vanished. A lot of things I read on the web have," he said, explaining that there's also a lot more self-censorship.

Despite this gloomy picture, Tel is not completely disparaging of China. "China is totalitarian but it's also not," he said "There are elements of freedom within the country too. Corrupt officials do get prosecuted now and again, for example."

This nuanced take is also visible in his story below, which includes scenes with a Taiwanese production company that cancel the shows, in their case because they're not profitable. This was an important addition for Tel.

"There's censorship by the government in China and commercial censorship in Taiwan, so people are not fully free to make TV shows in either countries," he told Index. As for his own stories, Tel doesn't believe they'll get published in China for the foreseeable future, even though their content is not especially controversial.

Time travel TV was chaotic. The Chinese Communist Party only want their narrative of the past

"I describe complex people doing their best," he added. But complexity, sadly, doesn't always make the cut in China. ⊗

Jemimah Steinfeld is the deputy editor of Index on Censorship magazine

The illegal time traveller

IT IS THE summer of 1839. The camel caravan appears in a dusty long-shot and tracks nearer and nearer, until it arrives at a gate in the ancient walls of Beijing. The imperial guards in the Fox Tower order it to halt, in order to inspect the cargo. The column of camels kneels and from one of them a figure draped in an indigo robe clambers down. He sways on the ground as if still riding on his beast, which wrinkles its lip at him. He reaches into a hidden pocket and pulls out a small shiny object, which he smiles at. It is a Huawei smartphone. He holds it up, for the sake of product placement. It should be displaying the name and logo of the show, but the screen is blank.

He pushes forward through the crowd. "My name is Song," he tells a fat man with a hairless face. "I am a merchant from afar. Could you please direct me to the Forbidden City?" The person pulls out a small shiny object, a silver spigot, and he inserts it into his groin, by means of which he urinates against the wall.

"What's your problem?" the person squeals at the stranger. "Have you never seen a eunuch before?"

→ Song looks around desperately. This wasn't in his script. How come there is no voice shouting "Cut!"? When is this scene going to end?

* * *

In a conference room on the 17th floor of the National Administration for Radio, Film and Television, a high-ranking cadre is addressing a delegation of producers.

"A decision has been made on the highest level. It is no longer permissible to make TV shows in which characters travel back in time to bygone dynasties. They make changes to history, which is impossible, and this encourages superstitious belief. Furthermore, their opposition to authority, however well-intentioned, sets a poor example."

A producer calls out: "But there are a dozen series in production right now!"

Another producer objects: "Time travel is one of the most popular memes. If we cancel the shows, this could lead to frustration and public unrest! Not to mention a substantial loss to the studios!"

A third objection: "In our mini-series, the hero enables Qin Shihuang to unify China! What could be more patriotic than that?"

A fourth: "In ours, the time traveller founds the May 4th Movement, giving birth to modern China!"

The cadre swishes his hands as if swatting a fly. "The decision is irrevocable. Both the production and the publication of such material is forbidden henceforth! Time travel is banned!"

Another producer says weakly, "But we're filming a pilot for a new show. The hero has just arrived in the Beijing of 1839."

The cadre slams his fist on the desk. "That is somebody else's problem!"

* * *

Song is baffled. The show had a modest budget. How come the set seems to extend so far? He trudges through alley after alley, with no obvious end. And how come there are so many extras, playing so many roles – beggars and prostitutes, kite-flyers and mahjong players, fortune tellers and quacks – plying their trade? The set seems huge and complex, built on the same scale as the Beijing of the period itself.

He knows roughly where he is, at least relative to the modern city. The ancient wall →

→ corresponds to what would be the Second Ring Road and a major subway interchange. According to the script, in the next scene he'd be in an establishing shot next to the Forbidden City. Well, he'll just have to walk there on his own. If he heads north, toward where the Marriot Hotel will be, and then west a couple of kilometres … But the road is blocked by a unit of the imperial guard. A fish ball seller remarks to him: "They're checking everyone. There's a rumour a foreign spy is in town. He's said to be wearing an indigo robe, much like yours." A guard shouts, "Hey! There he is!" and tries to grab Song by the braided queue at the back of his head, but the entire wig comes off in the guard's hand.

None of this was in the script. Song tries to run back the way he came. He heads down a side street, squeezing between carts and rickshaws. His only hope is to find his time machine and return to the present day. There it is, where he left it, beside a tavern. It is disguised as a palanquin, resting on the ground. A group of old men are gathered beside it, comparing their cage birds. Song shoves past them; he pulls back the curtains and enters.

From inside, it seems larger. There's an app on his smartphone that should sync with the time machine. He double-clicks on the icon. Nothing happens. Damn, he'll have to operate the time machine the old-fashioned way. He rotates a brass ship's wheel and spins a lever like

He pulls back the curtain, hoping to find himself on the backlot of the TV company in modern Beijing, but he remains in 1839

a starting handle. He gives the machine a good kick. It whines like a mosquito. The palanquin shudders and he feels a sensation something like being in the spin-cycle of a washing machine and something like swallowing himself feet-first… He pulls back the curtain, hoping to find himself on the backlot of the TV company in modern Beijing, but he remains in 1839. The bird aficionados are still gathered outside. A figure in a civil servant's embroidered surcoat beckons to him.

"I've not rehearsed this scene," Song says.

"Things not working out for you? Yearning to escape? Follow me!"

The civil servant guides Song into the backroom of what appears to be a vegetable shop. He points to a mat on the floor and gestures that Song should lie down. Then the civil servant displays a small lacquered casket, which opens to reveal a sticky black substance. He dips a wire in it and lights a sulphur match. He holds a long pipe and Song sucks on the mouthpiece and inhales the narcotic smoke.

Time shifts and wrinkles. Song relaxes; the Qing dynasty, the People's Republic - all merge into one …

He becomes aware another man is lying on the mat next to him. This man reaches into a pocket and pulls out a small shiny object, a Samsung smartphone, and taps away on it.

Song says, "You're a time traveller too? I thought I was the only one. When are you from?"

"2017."

"Me too!"

"My name's Tang. You tell me your backstory and I'll tell you mine."

"At the opening of the show," Song says, "I'm a nerdy physics teacher in a Beijing high school and I have a crush on a glamorous history teacher, who's obsessed with the Qing dynasty. In order to win her heart, I build a time machine, and promise to take her to her favourite epoch. But somehow we've lost each other. I'm not exactly sure what happens in subsequent episodes, but I'm pretty sure I'll show my valour by repelling the British imperialists and winning the Opium War. The history teacher and I are destined to live happily ever after. What about you?"

"You're quite the romantic hero, aren't you?" Tang grins. "I'm a comic fool. I get drunk at Spring Festival and stumble into what I think is my Toyota Corolla, but is actually a time machine parked by a visitor from the future, and accidentally I drive off in it. I find myself in a new dynasty every episode. I get into scrapes. I've already been in the Shang, Zhou and Han dynasties, and here I am in the Qing! The fellow who's serving us the opium, he's my sidekick. He's reincarnated in all my episodes."

Song says: "My time machine doesn't seem to work."

Tang chuckles: "It's never going to! Haven't you heard? Your government has banned time travel! You're stuck here!"

"What!?" Even in his befuddled state, Song is alarmed. "What do you mean, "your government"? And why do you speak Chinese in that weird accent, like your tongue won't curl back properly? Where are you from?"

"I'm from the Republic of China, of course. Taiwan."

"Oh no! I can't have a conversation with a Taiwanese! I could get into big trouble!"

"Take it easy!" Tang says, "Nobody's going to notice. Besides, in 1839 we're on the same side, both trying to help China win the Opium War, right?"

"Yes, but –"

"We time travellers should stick together. I'm the only one who can help you."

The two men walk through to the yard where Tang's time machine, which does indeed bear a strong resemblance to a Toyota Corolla, is parked. Song gets in the passenger seat. Tang turns the key in the ignition and releases the brakes. "2017! Here we come!" He laughs, "Oops! I've gone too far into the future." He shifts to reverse gear and the time machine beeps.

* * *

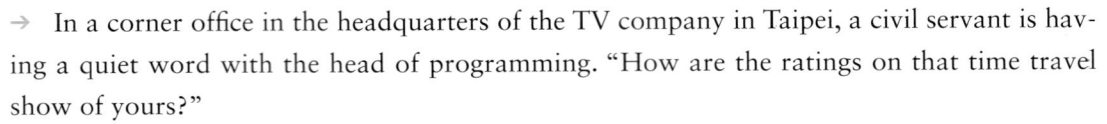

→ In a corner office in the headquarters of the TV company in Taipei, a civil servant is having a quiet word with the head of programming. "How are the ratings on that time travel show of yours?"

"Not so good. They've been dropping a little. We're trying to jazz it up."

"Drunkenness and now illegal drugs too! It sets a bad example."

"Opium isn't illegal in 1839."

"Even so."

"Plus it's educational. A history lesson. The moral being: maybe there are some problems nowadays, but things were a lot worse before the Kuomintang took charge!"

"And did you have to make the opium dealer a civil servant?"

"We had a spare costume left over from some other period drama. Rather a fetching outfit, with a pheasant embroidered on the sleeve of his surcoat, no?"

The civil servant clears his throat. "I understand your channel is in the red. In addition to my governmental work, I also assist a company which is looking to provide alternative programming. Lower cost, less risk and increase your profit margin. Drama, reportage, children's programming, who needs any of it?"

"What's the deal?"

"Replace the channel with a shopping network. More rewarding for the shareholders and I think we could arrange it so there's something in it for you personally."

The men shake hands. "When do we shift to the new format?"

"At once!"

"But the time traveller has just –"

"That is somebody else's problem."

* * *

Tang laughs. "My time machine has suddenly stopped working!"

"I don't see what's funny about that," Song says. "What on earth can we do!?"

"We'll just have to get out and see what's going on now."

"When are we?"

Tang peers at the dashboard chronometer. "The future. Let's find out what it's like."

Jonathan Tel is the 2016 winner of The Sunday Times EFG Short Story Prize. He has written both novels and short stories and has been published in The New Yorker and Granta

A tale of two Peters

Controversial Russian author **Alexei Tolstoy**, nicknamed the Comrade Count, was a prominent writer during the early Soviet period, despite not always writing favourably about those in power. **Boris Dralyuk** introduces an extract from Tolstoy's short story Peter's Day, translated into English for the first time

FEW AUTHORS ASSOCIATED with the pre-revolutionary regime, and especially those of noble origin, adapted so well to Soviet life and literary culture as Alexei Tolstoy. But this wasn't the case from the start.

Born into a prosperous and literary family in 1882, Alexei was a remote relative of the more famous Leo Tolstoy (and a descendant of Peter Andreyevich Tolstoy, who appears in the story overleaf). He published his first story in 1908, and soon developed a reputation both as a gifted craftsman of prose and an essentially apolitical bon vivant. During the civil war in the wake of the 1917 October

ABOVE: Alexei Tolstoy (right) out for a walk with Maxim Gorky in January 1934

→ Revolution, Tolstoy sided with the monarchist White Russians. In 1919, Tolstoy escaped the advancing Bolshevik army via Odessa, winding up, along with hundreds of thousands of other Russian refugees, in Paris. He later realised he wanted to return home. After proving his bona fides by writing for a number of Bolshevik-friendly publications, he returned to Soviet Russia in 1923.

Although he started his Soviet career with experimental works in a number of popular genres, including the science fiction classic, Aelita, published the year he returned, he found his true métier in historical fiction. Peter the Great, his three-volume novel chronicling the emperor's life, won the acclaim of the Soviet leader Joseph Stalin. Perhaps unsurprisingly, Tolstoy's portrait of a fearless Russian moderniser appealed to a man then implementing his own radical policies of industrialisation and collectivisation. As the historian Robert C. Tucker puts it, Tolstoy's "Peter became the would-be Stalin of yesteryear, and his revolution from above the partial *piatiletka* [five-year plan] of early eighteenth century Russia".

But Peter the Great wasn't Tolstoy's first work about the monarch. In 1918, in the midst of the civil war, Tolstoy wrote a very different story tracing a single day in Peter's life, never before published in English. This Peter is a somewhat different type – a self-indulgent, drunken fanatic and sadist. In the scene below, which is based on an actual historical incident, he tortures Varlaam, one of the "Old Believers", a sect that split off from the Russian Orthodox Church, for preaching that he, Peter, is the Antichrist.

What Tolstoy's story dramatises is the personal interest – the downright pleasure – Peter took in crushing opposition and those who spoke against him, as well as the foolhardiness of his mission. This image of Peter as bloodthirsty tyrant, clearly inspired by the bloodshed of the civil war, is an uncensored moment of truth. It is a message in a bottle from 1918, which profoundly alters our impression of the glorified Peter in Tolstoy's later work. This is not the image of Peter that Stalin authorised, precisely because it is far closer to the leader Stalin actually was. Needless to say, this powerful story was not widely circulated in the Soviet Union at the time. ⊗

Boris Dralyuk is a literary translator and executive editor of the Los Angeles Review of Books. He is the editor of 1917: Stories and Poems from the Russian Revolution, and co-editor of The Penguin Book of Russian Poetry

Peter's Day

Varlaam had been hanging on the rack for 40 minutes. His arms – bound over his head and wrenched out at the shoulders – were strapped to a crossbar; his head was lowered and the matted strands of his hair obscured his face and tangled with his long beard; his naked, dirty, outstretched body, its ribs protruding, was stained with blotches of soot and drying blood trickled down his side: Varlaam had just received 35 lashes of the knout, and the front of his body had been burnt with birch brooms. His dirty feet, their toes seized with spasm, were yoked together and fastened to a log. The executioner – a burly man in a short sheepskin coat – was standing on the log, stretching Varlaam's entire body.

At a table opposite the rack, seated before two candles that cast their light up at the brick vaults, was Tsar Peter – sprawled out, his head thrown back, the veins on his neck bulging; Peter Andreyevich Tolstoy in the middle; and, to the right of Tolstoy was a huge, sullen man with a red face like a lion's – Ushakov – who wore a fox fur hat with no wig and a velvet coat with a shaggy collar.

"Time to take him down? Might croak," Tolstoy said, looking over the testimony he had just recorded. Ushakov gazed at the hanging man without moving a muscle and wheezed through his throat, which was sore and choked with tobacco: "Give 'im a little vodka, he'll come to."

Tolstoy looked up at the tsar. Peter nodded. The executioner whispered into the darkness behind the pillars: "Vasya, Vasya, fetch that there bottle from the corner."

A round-faced, curly-haired fellow with a womanly mouth came out of the darkness, carefully carrying a four-sided bottle of vodka. He and the executioner pulled back the hanging man's head, bustled about for a while and stepped away. Varlaam groaned softly, then turned

You may take my body, Tsar, but I will get away. You may force me to crawl on all fours, put a bit in my mouth, take my tongue from me, say that my land is not my land, but I will get away

his head… Once again, as before, his black eyes glistened through the strands of his hair and fixed squarely on Peter. Tolstoy began to read out the record of the inquest. Suddenly Varlaam spoke in a voice that was weak but clear: "Beat me, torment me, I am prepared to answer for our Lord Jesus Christ before my torturers…"

"Shut your…" Ushakov tried to silence the man, but Peter grabbed him by the arm and leaned forward on the table, listening.

"I answer for all the Orthodox people. Tsar, there have been tsars more fierce than you. I am not afraid of fierceness!" Varlaam continued, taking breaks between words, as if he were reading from a difficult book. "You may take my body, Tsar, but I will get away. You may force me to crawl on all fours, put a bit in my mouth, take my tongue from me, say that my land is not my land, but I will get away. You sit on high and your crown is like the sun, but you will not seduce me with vain charms. I know you. Your time is short. I will tear the crown from your head and all your charms will be seen for what they are – foul smoke."

Peter parted his lips and spoke: "Your comrades, name your comrades."

"I have no comrades, no helpmates – all the people of Rus', they're my comrades."

→ The tsar's head bent forward, his mouth twisted violently and his cheek began to twitch; breathing loudly and clenching his teeth, he held the seizure back and overcame it. Ushakov and Tolstoy sat perfectly still in their armchairs. The executioner jumped on the log with all his might and Varlaam's head shot back. The candles crackled. At last Peter rose from his armchair, approached the hanging man and stood before him for a long time, as though deep in thought.

"Varlaam!" he pronounced and everyone trembled. The fellow with the womanly mouth stretched his neck from behind the pillar and gazed at the tsar with his gentle blue eyes.

"Varlaam!" Peter repeated.

The hanging man did not move. The tsar placed a palm on Varlaam's chest, over his heart.

"Take him down," he said. "Fix his arms. Prepare the needles for tomorrow."

[...]

Varlaam was led in and left alone with the sovereign. A little flame flickered in a saucer on the edge of the table. The logs on the hearth hissed, struggling to catch fire. Peter wore a fur

When Varlaam finished and fell silent, Peter, who was deep in thought, repeated several times: "I don't understand. I don't understand. Terrible mess. Drivel… Can't sort it out."

coat and hat. He sat deep in his chair, leaning his elbows on its arms and propping his head up with both hands, as if he had suddenly grown mortally tired. Varlaam stuck out his beard and gazed at the tsar.

"Who ordered you to speak about me?" Peter asked quietly, almost calmly.

Varlaam sighed and shuffled his bare feet. The tsar held out his palm: "Here, take my hand, feel it. I'm a man, not some devil."

Varlaam moved closer, but did not touch the hand.

"Can't lift my arms. They're tied," he said.

"Are there many like you, Varlaam? Tell me. I won't torture you now, tell me."

"Many."

Peter fell silent again.

"You read the old books, cross yourselves with two fingers? So, what does it say in those books of yours? Tell me."

Varlaam moved even closer. The chapped lips beneath his matted mustache parted several times, like those of a fish. But he didn't speak. Peter urged him again: "What's the matter? Tell me."

Varlaam lowered his inflamed eyelids, cleared his throat as though he were about to start reading and began to speak. Kirill's book warns, he said, that there shall be a proud prince in this world under the name of Simon-Peter and he shall be the Antichrist, and that the saviour's hand was not drawn in blessing at the general hall, and that the Blessed Virgin was drawn without an infant, and that the priests no longer had to serve over five prosphora, and that those priests were tearing up and trampling the new prayer books, which were written in shorthand and left out the words: "and the holy spirit"; and that there was great discord and much vanity among the lay folk, and that Count Golovkin's son had a red cheek, and that Fyodor Chemodanov's son, he had a black spot on his cheek and there was hair growing out of that spot, and it was said that such people would come in the time of the Antichrist.

Peter sat with his cheeks propped on his fists and seemed not to be listening. When Varlaam finished and fell silent, Peter, who was deep in thought, repeated several times: "I don't understand. I don't understand. Terrible mess. Drivel… Can't sort it out."

For a long time he stared at the burning logs. Then he got up and stood before Varlaam, looking huge and kind. Varlaam suddenly began to whisper and it looked as if his whole wizened face were laughing: "Oh, you, little father, little father of mine…"

Then, suddenly, the tsar bent down and clasped Varlaam by the ears, as if he wanted to kiss him. His hot breath, soaked through with wine and tobacco, poured over the prisoner's face. He looked deeply into Varlaam's eyes, muttered something, turned, pulled his hat down on his head and coughed: "Well, Varlaam, looks like we haven't settled on anything. I'll be back to torture you tomorrow. Farewell."

"Farewell, little father!"

Varlaam stretched towards him – as if Peter were his newfound father, as if he were a brother doomed to even greater torment – but Peter didn't turn around. He kept walking towards the door, which his broad back almost blocked from view.

Outside the gates, grasping the rail of his gig and stopping for a moment before getting in, he reflected that his day had ended, a day of work, grueling and drunken. And the weight of this day, as well as of all the days that preceded it and of all the days still to come, descended like lead onto his shoulders, the shoulders of a man who had assumed a burden beyond human strength: one for all.

Translated by **Boris Dralyuk**

Alexei Tolstoy *was a Russian writer active in the first half of the 20th century, who was most famous for his historical novels and some of the earliest science fiction in the Russian language. His books sold in the millions and became the base of several films. He died in 1945*

Index around the world

INDEX NEWS

46(02): 110/113 | DOI: 10.1177/0306422017716067

The Index awards bring attention to the dangers of reporting in the Maldives, while a new Index report reveals the precarious state of journalism in the USA, **Kieran Etoria-King** writes

INDEX AROUND THE WORLD

Zaheena Rasheed said that on the eve of finding out about the nomination, Maldives Independent staff had been questioning if they "were making a difference".

"The space for independent press in the Maldives was shrinking every day, but public apathy was growing," she added.

Index associate producer Helen Galliano, who organised the awards gala, said of Rasheed's speech: "It just showed how we are having an impact and how we're making a difference for her, for all of them. That was really incredible to hear."

The awards are part of a wider year-long fellowship programme. To launch the fellowship, the winners attended a week of workshops and meetings aimed at equipping them with skills to aid their work. For Galiano, a favourite moment came during a group lunch on the final day. The winners spoke of feeling loved, supported and rewarded.

Of the four winners, two were unable to attend due to their dissident status. Arts winner Wang Liming, a Chinese political

OPPOSITE:
Zaheena Rasheed, former editor of the Maldives Independent, delivers her speech after collecting her Index award in April

You can refuse to let these people silence me. Together, we can refuse to look away

"**THIS AWARD REALLY,** for us, feels like a lifeline," said Zaheena Rasheed, winner in the journalism category at the Index Freedom of Expression Awards 2017. In her acceptance speech, Rasheed, who was formerly editor of the Maldives Independent, spoke of the difficulties of being a journalist in that country. The newspaper's recent reporting of corruption, crime and religion has led to the arrests of all its staff. One colleague, Ahmed Rilwan, has been missing for nearly three years and Rasheed herself is now living in exile in Doha. A few days after the awards, her friend and fellow writer Yameen Rasheed was murdered.

cartoonist better known as Rebel Pepper (see page 101 for one of his cartoons), has been in exile in Japan since 2014, while winner of the campaigning category Ildar Dadin, recently released after a two-year prison stint for staging one-man protests in Russia, was unable to get a visa to travel. In a speech read by his wife Anastasia Zotova, who collected the award from human rights campaigner Bianca Jagger on his behalf, he said: "You can refuse to let these people silence me. Together, we can refuse to look away."

The digital activism award went to Turkey Blocks, an organisation that tracks shutdowns of internet access in the →

CREDIT: Elina Kansikas

111
INDEXONCENSORSHIP.ORG

ABOVE: A photographer is confronted by a police officer while covering protests during Trump's inauguration in January 2017

country. Turkey Blocks' success has seen its founder Alp Toker expand the project to track similar abuses elsewhere.

"Online censorship is increasingly used to mask more severe human rights violations, not just in Turkey but from China, Vietnam, Pakistan, India [and] Kashmir to Cameroon and Bahrain and all over the world," Toker said at the awards. "As long as freedom of

It's routine for journalists who are going to cover a protest to be swept up by the police

expression and digital rights are not safeguarded, our mission will continue."

Away from the awards, Index turned its attention to the USA with the publication of a report called It's Not Just Trump: US Media Freedom Fraying at the Edges. Using the methodology of its Mapping Media Freedom platform, which tracks violations of media freedom around Europe, Index researched more than 150 incidents, including border detainments, arrests and physical violence against journalists. Index's Sean Gallagher, editor of the report, said its creation was motivated by a desire to officially log the frequent violations to the media that Index staff had been aware of during the 2016 presidential election. Gallagher was shocked by the number of journalists being arrested and charged while covering protests.

"When I started out in journalism in the USA in 1993, this wasn't something that happened," said Gallagher, who is from New York. "Sure, there were fringe cases you can point to, but not on the scale that we're seeing now, where it's routine for journalists who are going to cover a protest to be swept up by the police. That's something that's new."

The report also found journalists were increasingly facing attacks from members of the public, with video journalists having their equipment stolen – sometimes at gunpoint – and being menaced by protesters accusing them of misrepresentation. In one case study, a documentary-maker working on a film in support of fracking was surrounded by protesters and had to be escorted away by police. In another case, a passer-by spat into a journalist's camera lens.

Gallagher believes this is caused by the skewed consumption of social media and online news, which has led to people across the political spectrum to seeing their own point of view as the only legitimate one.

"I think that people have come to expect that their point of view is going to be represented and they're unhappy when it's not represented to their satisfaction." He added: "Trump is not the main catalyst for it; Trump is capitalising on it, but it's a trend that's been there."

The full report is available to read at indexoncensorship.org. Index will continue to monitor press freedom in the USA, teaming up with the Committee to Protect Journalists, the Freedom of the Press Foundation, the Reporters Committee for the Freedom of the Press and the Knight First Amendment Institute at Columbia University for a collaborative project called US Press Freedom Tracker.

In another collaborative effort, Index marked World Press Freedom Day on 3 May by taking part in a vigil with other organisations outside the Turkish embassy in London to protest against Turkish President Recep Tayyip Erdogan's ongoing crackdown on the media. At the end of April, 163 journalists were in jail in Turkey, according to the Platform for Independent Journalism (P24). Ryan McChrystal, assistant online editor at Index, said: "Protesting is something that comes easily to us and so we often take that right for granted. But in Turkey, showing dissent is now a very dangerous thing to do. On World Press Freedom Day, we sent a message to the Turkish government that we are watching and their abuses of power have not gone unnoticed. More importantly, we gathered to send a message of solidarity to those imprisoned or persecuted."

Index has supported censored writers in Turkey through Turkey Uncensored, an online project. It has published articles from a range of writers, including ousted Cumhuriyet editor Can Dündar.

At the end of May, Index went to Wales to take part in Hay Festival. Magazine editor Rachael Jolley spoke on a panel called The War on Women alongside journalist and author Christina Lamb, human rights lawyer Baroness Helena Kennedy and Baroness Joan Bakewell. Deputy editor Jemimah Steinfeld hosted a conversation with Canadian novelist Madeleine Thien, who was shortlisted for the 2016 Man Booker Prize for her novel Do Not Say We Have Nothing. The two discussed censorship in China, past and present.

"Hay is basically a music festival for literature and literature can't thrive without free speech. This makes Hay a natural partner for Index," Steinfeld said of the ongoing relationship between the two organisations.

Kieran Etoria-King is editorial assistant at Index. He is the current Liverpool John Moores/ Tim Hetherington fellow, spending a year working on the magazine and website

LEFT: The cover of Index on Censorship's report on US media freedom

CREDIT: Mobilus in Mobili/Flickr

What the Romans really did for us

END NOTE

Far from being original, today's propaganda builds on a rich history of the dark art, writes **Jemimah Steinfeld**

THE EU'S POLICE agency, Europol, recently revealed evidence that Isis is creating its own social media platform for the purpose of disseminating propaganda. It may be connected to Facebook and Google ramping up efforts to curb extremist material and "fake news". In May, according to Reuters, Europol director Rob Wainwright said it showed "some members of Daesh, at least, continue to innovate in this space". But while technological innovation might still be possible, will there be anything original on this new platform?

A striking image, a catchy phrase, shocking material – these are the bread and butter of propaganda. It turns out these tactics stretch right the way back through history. From etchings in caves to the Bayeux Tapestry, pushing out messages that seek to persuade and influence – the basic definition of propaganda – is as old as mankind. There was one figure, though, who really cracked it.

"Augustus is probably the supreme master of the art of propaganda in the entire history of the West. No one has rivalled him and everyone has since been in his shadow," said historian Tom Holland, author of bestselling books on Rome, in an interview with Index on Censorship magazine.

Until the reign of Augustus, no one in Rome had come close to creating a personality cult. Rome was built on the idea that it was a republic and that no single man should dominate all others. When Caesar's vanity led to his face appearing on coins, his demise quickly followed. Augustus, coming straight after Caesar, used hindsight to his advantage. He cast himself as essentially a normal person, even adopting the title *princeps* (first citizen), and would partake in entertainment with the masses, like racing, boxing and watching gladiators. But he also positioned himself as exceptional, using the title *divi filius* (son of the god), and his portraits echoed those of Apollo. Augustus's face was everywhere, from statues, friezes and coins to writings and poems, and most famously in his appearance in Virgil's Aeneid.

"He promotes himself with absolute genius," Holland said. "He is simultaneously a figure who is an everyday guy and a figure of supernatural potency… he appeals to every aspect."

Augustus perfected propaganda and his influence on Napoleon, Mussolini and Hitler can be seen clearly. The careful crafting of Mao's image – clad in a simple "Mao suit", with sunbeams resonating off his body – was straight out of the Roman ruler's playbook.

CREDIT: Albert/Flickr

END NOTE

So Augustus provided the template, but technological change has undoubtedly improved the means. The birth of the modern printing press was a godsend for propaganda. It was during World War I, when there was a need to recruit, that Wellington House in London established a secret propaganda bureau, and from this the political poster was born. Driven by similar motives. President Woodrow Wilson in the USA formed the committee on public information, which produced posters, films and other material that sought to champion home security and democracy against a foreign enemy. The →

ABOVE: A statue of Emperor Augustus, exhibited at the Grand Palais in Paris, 2014

115
INDEXONCENSORSHIP.ORG

committee attempted to convince millions of people that they should support the war, and those that still rallied against it, such as socialist publications, were silenced in the process.

The demands of the Russian Revolution quickly gave birth to a whole new genre, Socialist Realism or constructivism ("production art"), in which smiling peasants and strident factory workers were portrayed in bold colours and geometric shapes, pithy slogans slapped on top. Anatoly Lunacharsky, who was in charge of the People's Commissariat for Education shortly after the Bolsheviks took charge, believed that by depicting the perfect Soviet man, art could create perfect Soviets.

Propaganda did not work just on what was shown; it worked also on what was

Augustus is probably the supreme master of the art of propaganda in the entire history of the West

omitted. Stalin was a master of this. Long before the advent of Photoshop, technicians in Russia manipulated photos so much that they became outright lies. David King, in The Commissar Vanishes: The Falsification of Photographs and Art in Stalin's Russia, wrote that during the Great Purges, in the 1930s, "a new form of falsification emerged. The physical eradication of Stalin's political opponents at the hands of the secret police was swiftly followed by their obliteration from all forms of pictorial existence". The book highlights classic cases of "now you see me, now you don't". It includes series of images featuring the same backdrops but with rotating casts, depending on who was or wasn't in favour at the time.

"At the heart of authoritarian propaganda is the manipulating of reality. The authoritarian must undermine this," said Yale philosophy professor Jason Stanley, author of How Propaganda Works, in an interview with Index.

The birth of mass media meant that propaganda didn't need to confine itself to unmoving imagery. Instead, people's minds could be influenced in a far more interactive way. Lenin called the radio "a newspaper without paper… and without boundaries" and used it to promote the Bolshevik message. And the revolution was televised, first at the cinema and then on TV. Sergei Eisenstein's most famous films – October, Battleship Potemkin and Alexander Nevsky – were huge successes precisely because they fused technical brilliance with politically correct storylines.

The myriad possibilities of propaganda were not lost on Hitler, either. He devoted two chapters of Mein Kampf to it and, once in power, recruited a minister of propaganda, Joseph Goebbels, who declared that with enough repetition and understanding of the human psyche, people could be convinced that a square was a circle.

Propaganda once again changed with the advent of the internet as information, or misinformation, could be spread with a simple click. Yet even though the game has moved on, the rules remain the same. Whether it's a fabricated blog post, a viral video of North Korea bombing Washington or tirades of tweets telling everyone you're going to Make America Great Again, these are all timeless tactics repackaged for the modern day.

"Everything you read in the newspapers, it's age-old," said Stanley, who added that "tech people" see this as a modern problem that they can solve. People are misinformed about the past, he said.

Misinformed, yes, but also manipulated by people and industries that can look to history's masterminds for best practice when it comes to propaganda. ⊗

Jemimah Steinfeld is deputy editor of Index on Censorship magazine